Master Evernote

The Unofficial Guide to Organizing Your Life with Evernote

(Plus 75 Ideas for Getting Started)

By S.J. Scott

http://www.HabitBooks.com

July 2014
Copyright © 2014 S.J. Scott
All rights reserved worldwide.

Published by Archangel Ink
ISBN 1500527378
ISBN-13: 978-1500527372

Disclaimer

Your Free Gift

As a way of saying *thanks* for your purchase, I'm offering a free report that's exclusive to my book and blog readers.

Lifelong habit development *isn't* easy for most people. The trick is to identify what you'd like to fix and create a step-by-step strategy to make that change. The key is to know *where to start*.

In *77 Good Habits to Live a Better Life*, you'll discover a variety of routines that can help you in many different areas of your life. You will learn how to make lasting changes to your work, success, learning, health and sleep habits.

This lengthy PDF (over 12,000 words) reviews each habit and provides a simple action plan. You can download this free report at:
http://www.developgoodhabits.com/FREE

Table of Contents

The Importance of the Evernote Habit

Once upon a time, you needed filing cabinets and great organizational skills to keep up with the paperwork for every aspect of your life. And often, you had to maintain a series of notebooks to remember important facts, thoughts and random pieces of information.

With the advent of *Evernote,* those days are now in the past. What this tool provides is the perfect idea capture mechanism, plus a place to store all your important documents.

Modern day life can be overwhelming. With the Internet, social media, email, PDFs and assorted paperwork, we're constantly bombarded with an unprecedented amount of information. Yes, knowledge is more accessible than ever before, but this information can be overwhelming if it's not properly filtered and maintained.

As an example, how often have you remembered seeing something important, but couldn't recall exactly *where* you saw it? Then you end up spending minutes—even hours— scouring your hard drive, scrolling through bookmarks and searching through old emails just to find one link or piece of information. Talk about a complete waste of time.

The truth is we're inundated with too much to do. Ideas, television shows, social media networks and advertisements supply so much "noise" that it's hard to slow down and keep track of the things that are truly important.

Fortunately, Evernote *does* provide a solution.

What you get with Evernote is a central location to store every thought, document and plan for the future. This tool will help you organize your life so you never worry about losing a valuable piece of data. You'll learn how to get organized in this book – *Master Evernote: The Unofficial Guide to Organizing Your Life with Evernote.*

About "Master Evernote"

While reading this book, you will learn how to make Evernote an essential part of your everyday life. Not only will you learn the basics of this tool, you'll also discover a framework for developing the "Evernote Habit" for organizing your daily activities.

My challenge is to teach you something valuable— regardless of your previous experience with Evernote. Some readers will already know the basics of Evernote, while others will have no clue about how it works.

As a result, this book will be broken down into three different sections. The first includes an exhaustive "how to" that explains everything you need to know to maximize your experiences with Evernote.

While this information is useful for the brand new Evernote user, experienced people might feel it doesn't cater to *their* needs. When writing this book, I had to act on the assumption that some readers don't have any

experience using Evernote, so the first section is designed
to give beginners a crash course on the app.

That said, there are a lot of great nuggets buried in the
"how to" section—even for experienced Evernote users. I
recommend reading those sections or at least skimming
through them to see you if can pick up a new trick or two.

The next section covers a few *advanced* strategies. These
strategies are little-known tactics that can take your
Evernote experience to the next level.

Finally, the third section gives 75 ideas for using
Evernote to organize all aspects of your life. These
recommendations run the gamut from simple strategies to
advanced "hacks" even the most avid Evernote users don't
know.

I cover a lot of information in this book. It's my hope
that every reader—no matter your experience level with
Evernote—will learn a number of things and apply them
immediately.

About Me

My name is S.J. Scott. I run the blog Develop Good
Habits (http://www.developgoodhabits.com/).

The goal of my site is to show how *continuous* habit
development can lead to a better life. Instead of lecturing
you, I provide simple strategies that can be easily added to
any busy life. It's been my experience that the best way to
make a lasting change is to develop one quality habit at a
time.

One area I'm always trying to improve is my personal
productivity. The way I figure things is, the better I become
at managing time, the more time I'll have to relax and enjoy
life. As a result, I'm always looking for ways to better
organize my life. After using Evernote for the past six

months, I know Evernote is an ideal tool for organizing all of the things I do on a daily basis.

About the "Evernote Habit"

There's a reason why my site is called Develop Good *Habits*. I believe the key to success with *anything* is to turn it into a daily habit. The same goes for using Evernote. The more you use this tool on a daily basis, the more you'll get out of it.

Throughout this book, I supply tools, ideas and action plans to help you get results with Evernote. There's enough information to turn you from a basic user into an advanced power user. However, you *still need* to develop the habit of using this tool as part of your everyday life. This means you should consciously remind yourself to use this tool—until it becomes an ingrained habit.

If you need reinforcement, then I recommend using a "habit accountability" app such as Lift.do or even creating a reminder within Evernote to check in every day. Don't worry; I'll show you how to do this in a bit. There's a lot to cover, so let's get to it.

Evernote Defined (and Four Reasons to Use It)

Odds are, you've already heard about Evernote, but maybe you're not sure what it is, why people like it or why you should use it on a daily basis. So to kick things off, let me start with the basics of this tool.

Evernote is a software suite designed to help you archive important documents, bookmark websites and take extensive notes. Evernote also makes it easy to keep track of Web clippings, voice memos, photos, handwritten notes and timed reminders

Another important feature of Evernote is it syncs across all your devices. This means you can add items on your desktop and then instantly access them on your mobile phone or tablet.

I like to think of Evernote as a single source for a paperless office. No piles of papers. No filing cabinets. No hours wasted looking for one piece of information. What Evernote gives you is a central place for every important document and bookmark.

Sound like a tool you'd like to use?

If so, here are four major benefits of Evernote:

Benefit 1: Capture Every Thought and Idea

Ideas come and go. If you don't write them down, they may be gone forever. We've all had that experience where we rush to find a pen and paper to write down an important thought. The problem with this method? It's hard to be organized if you're buried under a pile of random ideas.

In *Getting Things Done*, David Allen talks about the importance of having a "ubiquitous idea capture device." Without a doubt, Evernote is the perfect device for recording and sorting every thought that pops into your head. No matter where you are (either on your phone or in front of your computer), you can open Evernote and quickly create a quick note or make a short audio file.

Benefit 2: Improve Your Daily Organizational Efforts

We all wear different hats: parent, spouse, employee, athlete, or hobby enthusiast. Each of these titles comes with a variety of responsibilities. This means you need to maintain information related to the different aspects of your life. You might want to keep your favorite recipes separate from your work presentation notes, however.

What Evernote provides is a simple interface that lets you easily organize information related to your various interests. More importantly, with its tags and search features, you can easily retrieve every important piece of information when you need it (more on this later).

Benefit 3: Access on Multiple Platforms

I have two laptops, a smartphone and an iPad. Each is used at random times and for different reasons. But no matter what device I'm on, there are moments when I need to write down something important. What I love about Evernote is its simple syncing feature. When you add a file, it is immediately accessible on all platforms.

Benefit 4: Go Paperless

When you use Evernote to organize documents, ideas, receipts, statements, to-do lists and other information, you decrease the amount of clutter in your life. Ultimately, this could be your first step to living a paperless existence.

Plus with CamScanner, you get an app that works perfectly with Evernote. Basically you can turn any smartphone into a portable scanner that digitizes your documents and saves them to your Evernote cloud.

Now, I'll admit that I haven't converted to a fully digital lifestyle. That's because I prefer to have "hard copy" versions of my to-do lists and project lists available during my work day. But I have found Evernote to be extremely useful in my journey toward cutting down on the level of paper clutter in my life.

Getting Started with Evernote

At this point you understand the core benefits of Evernote. So how do you get started? Because Evernote is a cross-platform tool, there are several ways to download it. To get started, use one of the following four links to instantly download the software suite:

- Web version: https://www.evernote.com/Registration.action
- Android: https://play.google.com/store/apps/details?id=com.evernote

- iPhone/iPad: https://itunes.apple.com/us/app/evernote/id281796108?mt=8
- Kindle: http://www.amazon.com/Evernote-Corp/dp/B004LOMB2Q

When you first start the app, you're presented with a choice that might be confusing. In the next section, we'll talk about what this is and how to know what's best for you.

Evernote Free vs Evernote Premium

You have two options with Evernote: use the free option or pay for the premium version. How do you know what's right for you? In my opinion, the free version *should be* good enough for most people when getting started. However, if you reach the point where you use it all the time, then you should consider upgrading to the paid version.

With that in mind, let's take a look at what you get when you upgrade to the premium version:

• Increased Monthly Uploads. Evernote free and premium both have unlimited storage, but the accounts differ by how much can be uploaded every month. Free has a limit of 60MB, while the premium version has a whopping 1 GB upload limit—enough for most of your files, high-resolution photos and audio recordings.

• Supersized Notes. The free version of Evernote has a limit of 25MB. No text file will take up this much space, but if you upload large files such as photos, videos or audio clips, you might want to consider the 100MB that comes with the premium option.

- Increased Notebooks. The number of notebooks you're given increases from 100 to 250.

- Increased Inbound Emails. The free version has a limit of 50 messages per day, but the premium version has a limit of 200.

- More Collaborative Options. In the free version, others can view your notes, but they cannot edit your notes. With the premium version, you have the option of allowing others to update your notes, making this a great tool for collaborative team projects.

- Priority Support. Like anything else in life, you get what you pay for. Premium members get quicker support if they have a problem or question about this app.

- Offline Notebooks. A great option for the business traveler. Offline notebooks allow you quicker access to your notes, even when a connection is not available for your mobile device. This also makes it easy to make updates to your notes when wireless access is not available (like during a plane flight).

- Passcode Lock. This is an additional layer of security if your files contain sensitive or other important pieces of information.

- PDF Annotation. The premium version allows you to make annotations on PDFs via Evernote.

- Access to Penultimate Paper Styles. This gives you access to all the "paper styles" using the Penultimate add-on app.

- Text-to-Speech Capabilities. The premium version includes a text-to- speech option to read your documents aloud using Evernote Clearly (another app we'll discuss later).

As you can see, many of the options for the premium version are nice, but nothing that you can't live without. *My recommendation?* Don't worry about the premium version until you become an Evernote junkie and want to put this tool through its paces.

After selecting either the free or premium option, you're ready to dive in and start using Evernote. In the next few sections, we'll talk about the basic functions of this tool and how to start using it on a daily basis.

Evernote Basics: What You Get "Out of the Box"

Evernote can be overwhelming when you first open it, so in the next few chapters, we'll cover the major features and discuss how each is used.

Let's start by talking about what you'll see when first opening the app. I just opened a new Evernote account and took the following screenshot. As you can see, I added a few notebooks and stacks to fill it up. I also created my first note with a title and a few tags.

Here's how it looks:

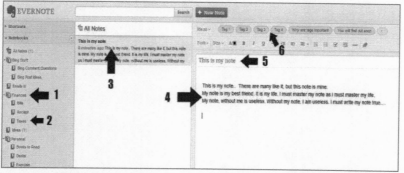

Note: This picture is the Windows version of Evernote. Things are laid out a little bit differently for a Mac, but all the same functions are present. Throughout this book, I use Windows layouts for most of my screenshots. In the cases where there is a substantial difference between the Mac and Windows versions, I show you both platforms.

Don't worry about the specifics of the individual features—each will be explained in more detail in the chapters to come. Instead, I want you look at the six arrows with numbers drawn on this image.

Each provides a unique feature that will help your overall experience with Evernote:

1. *Stacks* are collections of related notebooks.
2. *Notebooks* are a collection of notes.
3. *Notes* are the individual files within a given notebook.
4. The *body* of the note can be text, imported email messages, documents, PDFs, Web clippings, audio clips, photos or a combination of all of these.
5. The *title* simply acts as a shorthand reminder of the content of the note.
6. *Tags* help with searching and finding notes related to a particular topic.

Evernote revolves around creating notes and organizing them into different notebooks, stacks and tags. That's really the core idea behind this app. Evernote is simple to use, but there are things you can do with the software suite once you understand its basic features. As you read this book, you'll discover many ways to use Evernote to organize your life.

Okay, now that you know the core functionality of Evernote, let's talk about the one feature that will help organize your life.

Evernote Basics: Syncing Between Platforms

S yncing is my favorite feature of Evernote. You can update Evernote from your PC, get up, clip a few articles on your laptop, run out the door, grab a cup of coffee and then access these notes from your mobile device. Want to edit your notes on the go? If so, they will be updated automatically across all platforms. The best part? This entire process is done instantly without any thought or actions required on your end.

How does syncing work?

The Evernote program uploads all new and edited notes to the company's servers every 30 minutes by default. If you want to change the default setting, you can do so by selecting *Tools >> Options >> Sync*.

If you need to immediately access a new note on another device, then simply click the *Sync* button and it will upload the latest changes.

Important: You should always remember that mobile devices act differently when it comes to the syncing feature. Laptops and desktop computers will store a copy of everything on your hard drives. Unfortunately, mobile devices don't have the space needed to keep a hard copy of every file. This is an important difference for those who rely on Wi-Fi and want to access all their notes wherever they go.

Should You Back Up Your Notes?

Many Evernote users wonder if they should regularly back up their files. That really depends on your level of comfort with this app. Overall, synced notebooks are very safe, so you won't have to worry too much about backing up the files on a daily basis.

Here are a few reasons why.

Evernote is a huge company with more than 20,000 premium users and six million free users. They maintain a large number of servers to ensure data is as safe and secure as humanly possible. Quite frankly, they just can't afford to lose data and stay a successful business.

In addition, the data in Evernote is stored on your drives *and* in their cloud servers. So even if something *does* happen to one storage center, the other(s) should be safe. If you're like me and have multiple devices, you automatically have multiple places to back up your important files.

Yes, it's possible to lose a few minutes of work, but massive and catastrophic data dumps shouldn't be an issue.

Ultimately, the decision is up to you. If you want to store critical files on Evernote, then it makes sense to back up your files regularly. But if you're a casual user who uses this tool to create lists, capture ideas and bookmark important Web pages, then you won't have to worry too much about creating copies of your files.

Now that you understand the basics of Evernote and how syncing works, let's dive into actually *using* this tool.

Specifically, let's start with the core feature that you'll probably use on a daily basis—*Notes.*

Evernote Basics: Notes – The Building Blocks of Evernote

At this point, I recommend signing up for Evernote and downloading the free version. That's because the best way to learn *anything* is to practice it on a daily basis. My advice? Sign up and play with Evernote as you go through this book. Copy and paste a few things to your *Notes*. Make a few *Notebooks* and *Stacks*. Add *Tags* that represent your varied interests. In other words, use Evernote instead of simply reading about it.

One of the reasons Evernote is such a powerful application is because it makes it easy to add files and then retrieve them at a later date.

What can you put into Evernote?

Here are the types of files you can add to Evernote:

- Documents
- Personal notes
- Web pages
- Images
- PDF files
- Manuals

- Audio recordings

This is just the start of what you can do with Evernote. You can also mix the *types* of notes you use and create something with a deeper context. For instance, you can add a photo and include a few lines about where it was taken, who was there and why it's important for future reference. You can even use a tool like *Skitch* to mark up a picture and add important annotations (more on that later).

Regardless of the content, everything starts with a note, so let's talk about this core feature.

Notes: The Building Blocks of Evernote

A note is the core function of Evernote. With it, you can keep track of any information that's important to you. Simply think of anything you'd like to archive and add it to a note. Examples include business ideas, text messages, emails, pictures and important files. In the last part of this book, I'll provide 75 specific examples of *what* you can actually do with Evernote.

Like I said before, a note can be a picture, an audio file, written text or even a single word. You can create up to 100,000 separate notes for an Evernote account or dump everything into a single note. The only real "limit" to a note is the size of the individual file. For a free account, no single note can be more than 25MB and this size increases to 100MB for the premium option.

Honestly though, 25 MB is a lot of data. That is a few high-quality images taken with a high MP camera, or a very long piece of text. To give you some perspective, the file size of this book, which has more than 15 images, is only about 2MB. This means you can add a large amount of "stuff" to a note before worrying about its file size.

Notes: The Basic Layout

We've talked at length about what can be added to a note, so let's dive in and see how it looks on a desktop computer. Remember: This screen might look different depending on the specific platform you use to access Evernote.)

Here's a few things you can do with an individual note:

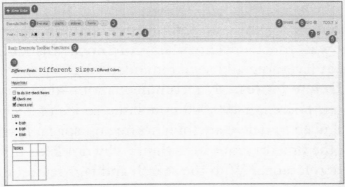

1. **New Note.** Use this button to manually create a new note.
2. **Notebook.** This scroll box shows the specific notebook where this note is stored (we'll get back to this feature in a bit).
3. **Tags:** This is an optional feature that allows you to create a label (or multiple labels) for the context of the note. This is an important feature that helps you search and find notes you created in the past.
4. **Editor Toolbar.** The editor function works like your average WYSIWYG (What You See Is What You Get) editor. If you look at the image, you'll see a variety of options including fonts, italics, bolding, indents and list formatting. You can also create simple tables and checkbox to-do lists.

5. **Share feature.** Send a note to email, Web addresses, Facebook or other third-party platforms with this option.

6. **Info.** This option provides additional functions for a note, which is important when using the premium feature and working with multiple authors.

7. **Set reminders.** You can set reminders with this option. Presets are single-button clicks for tomorrow and one week, but there's also a calendar function to set a reminder for any date and time in the future. Want to meet with friends twenty years from now? Just create a note in Evernote and set a reminder for 2034.

8. **Delete Notes.** My recommendation—don't use this option. There is a 100,000 note limit, so it's unlikely that you'll need to delete anything to free up space. If you took the time to write something, why not keep it for future reference? With the search and tags features, you can find what you want without wasting time shuffling through too many files.

9. **Title.** The title can be whatever you desire. If you don't use tags, make sure you create a tile that will help you remember the content of each note. This makes notes easier to locate. With the tagging option, a title becomes less important, since tags provide the best way to locate a specific note.

10. **Body of the note.** This can be a picture, an audio file, text or even just a single word. You can combine all these different options and import many notes as well.

I encourage you to review this section a few times. Try adding a few notes and playing around with the different features. You'll find that this tool is easy to use once you've done it a few times.

Notes: How Many is Too Many?

There's no limit to the amount of storage space that's offered with the Evernote Cloud. Really, the only limitations are the total number of notes you have and the monthly data upload limit.

One hundred thousand (100,000) notes is the hard limit for the free version of Evernote. But let's face it, 100,000 is a *lot* of notes. Even if you're like me and take notes on just about everything, odds are you won't hit this limit any time in the near future.

My point is this—you shouldn't worry about a specific note limit. Instead, you should think carefully about how you're organizing the notes and the speed with which you can find specific pieces of content. So as we move forward, the reason I recommend creating a strict organizational system is because you can quickly find anything—even if you have 100 *or* 100,000 notes.

Notes: Editing and Updating

One of the most versatile features of a note is the ability to edit and update from multiple platforms.

Let's say you've uploaded an Excel file into a note. You can open up the file, make changes, save it and it'll automatically update on Evernote. Then when you open up the same note on a different platform, the Excel file will also be updated.

The editing and updating aspect of Evernote is what makes it a great tool for collaborative efforts or anyone who likes to work from multiple devices.

Notes: Merging

Merging notes is not something you always want to do on the spot. For instance, you might take a quick picture that you'd like to edit later on. Perhaps you'd like to add other images or even a Web link. Each piece of information could be created as a separate note, but eventually you'd like to put them together into a single note.

Fortunately this is very easy to accomplish.

To merge notes:

• Choose the notes you wish to merge (Command + "Click" on Mac or "Ctrl + Click" on PC)

• A thumbnail view of the combined notes will appear with options to add tags, merge and move to different notebooks.

• Click the "Merge" button, which puts all the notes into a single file.

Easy, right? If you're someone who doesn't like too much digital clutter, the merge feature can help you streamline your Evernote experience and make it easier to organize multiple pieces of information.

Notes: How to Add an Image

Evernote allows you to upload and update pictures across all of your devices. This is a big part of why this tool is awesome—you can take a picture, sync it to Evernote and have it ready to edit using your favorite photo retouching software.

Here's how to add an image on different platforms:

Mac, Windows Desktop, and Evernote Web

1. Create a new note or open an existing note.
2. Drag the image from your computer into the note body OR use the paperclip ("Attach File") icon in the Evernote note editor to manually attach a file.

iPad, iPhone, and iPad Touch

1. Create a new note or open an existing note.
2. Tap the Paperclip or Camera icon.
   a. Choose Camera (take a new picture in Evernote)
   b. Choose Camera roll (add existing picture to Evernote)

Android

1. Create a new note or open an existing note.
   a. Tap the camera icon to capture a new photo from the Android device camera.
   b. Tap the "**+**" icon >> Attachment >> Pictures to attach an existing image from your camera roll.

Windows Phone

1. Create a new note or open an existing note.
   a. Press the camera icon button to take a new photo from your device's camera.
   b. Press the "**...**" icon to attach an existing picture from your camera roll.

Notes: How to Add Audio

I don't know about you, but my best ideas often come at random, even inconvenient, times. It's never when I'm sitting in my office. Instead, ideas pop up when I'm exercising, driving or running errands, and the *last thing* I want to do is stop to write down a lengthy thought. That's why the audio note option is helpful for remembering important ideas.

To record an audio note, simply stop what you're doing for a minute, open the Evernote application on your smartphone and record a quick audio reminder of your brilliant, life-changing idea.

Adding audio works similarly to how you add images:

1. Open a new or existing note.
2. Rather than clicking on the "paperclip" or the "camera" icon on your device, you click on the microphone icon or the "+" button for more options. While recording, you'll see a red icon. When you're done, simply stop the recording and save the file as a note.

It takes awhile to develop the habit of recording audio notes, but do this often enough and never again will you forget an important idea.

Notes: How to Add PDFs and Other Files

One of the last aspects of the notes feature is the addition of PDFs and other file extensions. The only limitation is the file size—no larger than 25MB (Free) or 100MB (Premium).

Adding other files is similar to adding audio files and images. Either drop and drag them into the note or insert them with the paperclip "Add File" button.

Notes: Additional Tips

As we close out the discussion on notes, there are a couple of additional tips to get the most from what you post on Evernote.

Tip 1. Use checklists for projects. One additional feature that's not available on many WYSIWYG editors is the "to-do list" feature. (This looks like a checkbox in the editor.) This feature lets you create list items and check them off by clicking your mouse or tapping your smartphone.

If you're using Evernote to manage projects, you can create a to-do list, print it out and easily check off all the tasks that need to be completed. You can also maintain this list on your smartphone and cross off each item as you work through a project. Using this feature is a great way to stay on top of important tasks.

Tip 2. Take many notes. The 25MB maximum size is a very large file, so you might be tempted to create huge notes with a lot of extraneous information. While this *could* work, I recommend taking lots of notes instead of dumping a ton of information into just a few notes.

One reason for this is the total upload limit. Whenever you edit a note and then re-upload it, the size of the <u>entire</u> note counts against the monthly limit—even if you only change one word.

For instance, let's say you write books and want to save them on Evernote. It would be wise to upload each chapter as a note, each book as a notebook, and all of your books as a stack.

Another reason is organization. Since you're using titles and tags to locate specific notes, it's not hard to find *anything*. But if an important piece of information is buried in a 20MB file, then it will take a *long time* to locate it.

Tip 3: Get an Alarm email. The "Alarm" feature will send you an email for a specific, pre-determined action. This is a great way to set a reminder for an important task or appointment.

Tip 4. Note encryption: Uploading any sensitive information to a cloud server is a scary proposition for some people. Chances are nothing will happen, but worrying about having your account hacked *after* it happens is like closing the barn door after the horse has been stolen.

Fortunately, the folks at Evernote provide an additional level of security beyond the standard account password. If you want to encrypt any part of a note, simply highlight the text that needs to be protected. Then "right click" or "tap" on the text, choose "Encrypt Selected Text," then enter the passphrase for decrypting the text.

A word of warning with this option: Evernote doesn't store your encryption key, so if you forget it, there's no way to recover the password. The only option you have is the password hint, which isn't helpful if it's something you don't normally use.

That's it for our discussion of the Notes feature. With what you've learned so far, you can immediately start using Evernote. Now that you have a firm grasp of this basic feature, let's move on and talk about how to organize *all* of your notes.

Evernote Basics: Notebook Mastery in Five Simple Steps

The *Notebook* feature is the core foundation of Evernote. With hundreds, thousands or even tens of thousands of notes, you'll need a consistent organizational hierarchy for your content.

Notebooks, which can include a single note or thousands of notes, are the first level of that structure. The important thing to remember is that each note can only be included in a single notebook. So if you have notebooks for @car, @bills and @repairs, you'll have to decide where to send the note marked *car repair bill*. The simplest solution to this "multi-category problem" is to use Tags, which we'll cover in a bit.

There is some debate on how to best organize notebooks. Some people like maintaining a lot of folders for the many different aspects of their lives. Others keep notebooks for only three or four key areas, and a few avoid notebooks entirely and organize everything with tags. Honestly, there are positives and negatives to each method, but my advice is to group everything according to the major areas of your life.

What's great about a notebook is it gives you a place to quickly store individual notes. However, when it comes time to find a note, it's better to create multiple tags and use these to find content.

Now that we've introduced the concept of the notebook, let's go over five steps to achieving mastery with this feature.

Step 1: Create a Default Notebook

There are dozens, even hundreds, of ways to import to files, audio recordings, Web clips, images and text into Evernote. Many of these can even be automated with the tools we'll discuss later on. To get started, though, I recommend creating a default notebook for any note you haven't organized and sorted.

If you don't set up a filtering system ahead of time, Evernote will automatically send every new note directly to a "default notebook" named after your user name. So if your user name is Steve, then "Steve's Notebook" will become the automatic dumping ground for all unlabeled Notes.

I strongly recommend changing the name of this notebook to something that is instantly recognizable, such as "Inbox" or "!Inbox" (*the special character in front of the word "!inbox" drives it to the top of any alphabetical display of notebooks*).

Step 2: Create Context-Specific Notebooks

A default notebook will only be effective until it gets cluttered with notes that don't relate to one another. A quick fix is to create a few context-specific notebooks for the different areas of your life. Don't worry; you can always edit these in the future, so this isn't an irrevocable action.

It's easy to create a new notebook. Simply right-click or tap on the "Notebooks" section on the left side of your

Evernote screen. Then select "Create Notebook" and create a name for this notebook. After that, decide if you want the notebook to be synchronized or local. Finally, tick the box if you want this notebook to be your default notebook.

Here's how this looks when I add a new Notebook called "Finances":

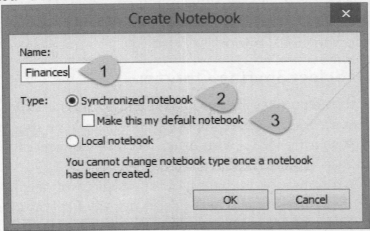

You might be confused about the choice between synchronized and local, so let's go over that in the next step.

Step 3: Choose Local or Synchronized Notebooks

Local Notebooks are only stored on the computer or mobile device you use to create them. This information is more secure since it's never uploaded to the Evernote cloud server. Since the primary benefit of Evernote is the syncing feature, I typically ignore this option. However, if security is of primary concern, then you might want to go with a local notebook.

Synchronized Notebooks are regularly updated on the Evernote cloud servers and subsequently downloaded to your other devices. By default, if you don't change your personal preferences, all notebooks will update every 30 minutes. If you want to immediately sync a file, click the sync button to instantly update the Evernote servers.

As you can see, notebooks come in two basic options. If you want instant access on all platforms, then choose the synchronized option. If you want to keep things secure, then select the local option.

Step 4: Select Sharing Options

Another feature of Evernote is it lets you give team members access to your notebooks. You also have the option of sharing URLs with others so they can access specific files or notebooks.

When a notebook is shared, other people can view it, but they can't modify it. There is also no way for you to edit the notes of other Evernote users. As we've discussed, the only unlock the editing feature is to purchase the premium version of Evernote, which allows you to edit and update notes and notebooks across multiple platforms and user accounts.

To get started with the sharing feature, simply open a note and select the "..." button on your smartphone or the "Share" button on a PC or Mac. From there, you can share content in a variety of ways: as a link, in an email, as part of a text message or via a social media account such as Twitter, LinkedIn or Facebook.

Step 5: Organize Your Notebooks

Now we come to the fun part—organizing your notebooks. The number of notebooks you have (or don't have) depends on your personal preferences. That said, there are a few "universal labels" you'll find useful in the journey toward using Evernote as an organizational tool:

!Inbox Notebook: The first folder to create is an !Inbox folder, which should be your default dumping ground for notes that haven't been organized into specific notebooks.

There are a few reasons you should create an !Inbox notebook.

First, keeping the notebook at the top of your list will remind you that you need to go through it on a daily basis to tag notes and move them to their proper places. With this *one habit*, you will build a simple system for organizing the hundreds—even thousands—of notes that you'll add in the future.

Another reason for using the !Inbox label is we've been trained over the years to treat an email inbox as the default dumping ground for unsorted messages. In a way, we have a Pavlovian response to sort and take action on these open loops. By labeling as the notebook "!Inbox," you'll piggyback on the pre-established habit of minimizing digital clutter.

!Action Notebook: Fans of David Allen and his *Getting Things Done (GTD)* method should have an !Action notebook. As with !Inbox, the special character preceding the word "Action" puts the notebook at the top of your list of options, so it instantly grabs your attention. (Later on, I'll go into more detail about how to combine GTD with Evernote.)

Even if you've never heard of David Allen, an action notebook makes a lot of sense. This notebook should only contain notes with specific, measurable tasks that need to be completed within a three-day window. My preference is to keep this list small (less than 10 items) and relevant to my priority projects for the week. Otherwise, all other action items should be a part of project list that you review on a weekly basis.

!Ideas: I recommend maintaining a separate notebook of ideas and spur-of-the-moment thoughts. This might include a combination of written notes, audio updates and context-specific photos.

My recommendation is to add to this notebook during the week. Then go through each item once a week during a review session. Explore each thought and decide if it's immediately actionable. If it is, then create a quick project list and schedule specific action items. If it isn't, then schedule a reminder to follow up on it at a later date. Finally, remove each note and file it in a long-term storage notebook called "Tickler File" or "Previous Ideas."

Random Notebook: Your Evernote program might be filled with random notes because you don't have time to sort them. It's okay put them in a temporary "Random" notebook until you have time to review them. The Tag feature makes it easy to find any note—even if it's in a disorganized pile of information.

That said, you should take the time to set up an organizational system for all aspects of your life instead of dumping everything into a random notebook. If you don't, you'll find yourself facing a pile of unsorted ideas, bookmarks and action items. My overall advice is to avoid stressing out if you slip up with the organization for a day or two, but you should put notes where they belong as often as possible.

If you end up creating a lot of notebooks, then you should consider taking your organizational efforts to the next level by building *Stacks*. In the next section, we'll talk about this feature and how it works.

Evernote Basics: Using Stacks to Organize Notebooks

S tacks are the third core organizational tool for Evernote. A stack is nothing more than a collection of themed notebooks based on the major "sections" of your life.

The folks at Evernote described stacks quite eloquently as *"digital dividers for your cloud-based filing system."* Before this feature was introduced, your only option was to create a laundry list of notebooks. If you had 10 to 15 notebooks, this wasn't a problem, but if you had 30 to 100 notebooks on a variety of topics, then it became a huge hassle to organize everything.

Ultimately, stacks allow you to take similar notebooks and put them in related groups.

They help create a cleaner, neater interface, which makes it easier to find any important piece of information.

As an example, my stacks include the following: Internet Business, Travel, Personal, Financial and Health.

Inside each stack is collection of different notebooks. For instance, my Internet Business notebook is has notes categorized with these labels: Kindle Publishing, Develop

Good Habits, Traffic Generation, Social Media and Books/Courses.

Try to limit your stacks to no more than 10 notebooks each. If you have too many, then find a few different themes for each stack and sort them a second time.

How to Create Stacks in Evernote

There are two primary ways to create a stack in Evernote.

The first is to drag one notebook on top of another notebook. This will group them together into another into a stack. You can then add a title of your choosing to the new group of notebooks.

The second method is to click a notebook that's not already in a stack. This gives you a few options. You can move it to a preexisting stack with "Add to stack" button or you can create a new stack by clicking the "New stack" option.

Here's how this looks:

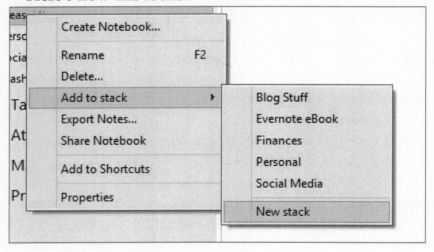

If you're visual person, then you should check out the official Evernote video on creating stacks: http://www.youtube.com/watch?v=p5STGsoHk2g

Now that you understand the basics of notes, notebooks and stacks, let's move on to what I consider to be *the* most important feature of Evernote—*Tags*.

Evernote Basics: Tags (and Why They're Important)

Tagging can be very time-consuming. When you first get started, it might seem like a hassle to create multiple tags for each note. Perhaps you might wonder why you should bother with it. Tags aren't important when you have 50 notes, but when you have 500 notes, 5,000 notes or even 50,000 notes, you'll need a good system for finding information without being forced to sort through dozens of notebooks.

What tags provide is a simple system for organizing and finding all of your information.

The first thing to know about tags is they're completely optional. I've already stressed their importance, but you don't "need" to tag a note before adding it.

That said, let me briefly go over why this feature helps you organize *everything* in Evernote.

Notebooks vs. Tags

Let me be clear here. The value of notebooks versus tags is subject to debate. While I'm a fan of tagging, others can make the valid argument that you'll be better organized by maintaining a large assortment of notebooks.

The people who are "against" tagging use Evernote like a classic filing system. Their stacks and notebooks provide a hierarchical method of organizing information. With this system, all they have to do is open a notebook (or stack) to find all information related to a specific topic.

The benefit of tags is you get an additional, lateral method of finding information. Think of it this way: if Evernote is like a filing cabinet, then a stack is an entire drawer and a notebook is similar to a folder with a lot of paperwork inside it. What tags give you is a shortcut for finding anything, *without* forcing you to open a drawer and waste time looking around.

Okay, I'll admit this might be hard to conceptualize, so here's a specific example.

I add a lot of pictures to a "Pinterest" notebook before posting them to the social media site. Without tags, I would have to scan through the entire folder to locate a certain picture. I could also do a search using the tag option (tag:Pinterest). However, since a note might have multiple tags (recipes, travel, business), it would be easier to find a photo using a multiple tag search (i.e. tag:Pinterest tag:recipes). This saves me from the hassle of scrolling through hundreds of pictures to find the one I want.

Another reason why tags are important is you're limited to a total of 100 notebooks with the free option, while the total number of notes caps out at 100,000. That means, theoretically, you could end up with 1000 notes for every single notebook. That's a *lot* to sort through just to find one item.

Fortunately, there is a limit of 100,000 per account, so you can add all sorts of identifiers to narrow down your searches and find things quickly.

When you take time to tag *and* create good notebook titles, you'll have two solid ways to locate everything.

As an example, let's say I needed to find a specific receipt. I could go to my *Finances* stack >> *Receipts* notebook or I could go to the Evernote search bar and type *tag:receipts* to display every note that's tagged with "receipts."

As you continuously add notes, I urge you to consider using both tags and notebooks. You may end up preferring one over the other, but until you've used Evernote for a bit, try both methods to see what works best for you.

Now that we've gone over the difference between tags and notebooks, let's talk about how to start adding tags.

How Do You Tag?

There are two ways to create a tag.

The first is when you create a new note. Depending on your device, you'd either select the "Click to add tag…" option or you'd select the *Note Details* button.

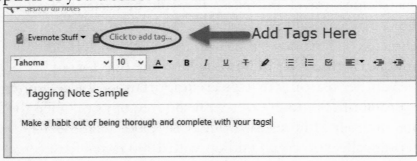

The second option can is available to those using a PC or Mac. On the left side of your computer, you'll see a list of tags. Simply click on the down arrow to add a new tag.

Here's how this looks:

That is all there is to creating tags.

I recommend using multiple tags for every note. In fact, you should create as many as 100 to 200 tags to match your varied interests. Yes, this will take some effort, but eventually you'll save time because Evernote "auto-populates" tags as you start typing a specific word.

For instance, when I'm adding a tag for a Pinterest image, as I type "P...i...n" Evernote will give me the option of selecting the "Pinterest" Tag. This means that once you've established a good system, it won't be hard to quickly add multiple tags to a note.

Tags take effort and dedication in the early stages, but when you have thousands of notes, you'll be glad you took the time to set up an organized system.

Now to maximize your experience with tagging, there are a few "best practices" you should follow, so let's talk about them.

Evernote Basics: 7 Best Practices for Tagging

There are no set rules for tagging, but I feel it's important to follow seven "best practices." Follow these guidelines and you can add *thousands* of notes without worrying about losing them in the mix. While *your* tagging rules might be different, the important thing to remember is you need to create some standardization within Evernote.

Here are seven best practices to consider.

Tagging Practice 1: Stick to a Standard Tagging Convention

Tagging one note as "Pic," another as "Pics" and a third as "Pictures" will wreak havoc on your ability to locate a specific photo. Be ruthless with using the same tag for similar notes.

Tagging Practice 2: Uses Plurals Instead of Singular Tags

Use the plural version of a word instead of its singular version. This makes it easier to find notes when you search for them.

If you type "picture" and the tag is "pictures," the note will show up since partial matches count. However, if I type "pictures" and the tag is "picture," the note won't show up because Evernote doesn't consider it to be the same word.

Do your best to be uniform with tagging. The good news is if you get this right for a few weeks, most of the tags you add will already be there when you need to tag a new note.

Tagging Practice 3: Tag with First Names and a Last Name Initial

There's nothing wrong with using someone's last name as a tag, but this practice can often lead to confusion. First of all, you have people like me who have last names that are also first names. Then there's the issue of tagging multiple family members. It can get confusing when you tag someone with a first name, last name or both names.

To avoid confusion, I recommend *always* tagging with a first name and an initial. If you have two people with same first names, it would look like "John C" and "John W."

Tagging Practice 4: Keep Tags Streamlined

The beauty of tagging is there isn't a realistic limit to how many you can have. Unfortunately, that's also the *danger* of tagging. Honestly, who really needs 100,000 tags?

Evernote can become very clunky if you have to sort through thousands of tags at the same time.

My point? Although you don't have to worry about reaching a hard limit, you shouldn't create a unique tag for every note. It's all a balancing act. Focus on being as descriptive as possible, but only use tags that correspond to the important areas of your life.

Tagging Practice 5: Start Broad, Then Narrow Your Focus

I like to start a note entry with a generic tag. These tags work great when they correspond to specific stacks or notebooks.

For instance, you could create tags like *Recipes*, *Travel*, *Health*, or *Home Improvement*. Then you should create additional tags that drill down into the specifics of the content. So, using the previous example, you could add to the *Health* tag using additional modifiers such as *Running*, *Lifting* and *Stretching*.

Tagging Practice 6: Identify the Who, What, Where, When and Why

A great way to create effective tags is to use the 5 W questions we all learned in school.

Let's discuss a concrete example here. If I tagged a photo of myself and four friends at the beach in Belmar, New Jersey, then my tags might look like this: *#belmar #newjersey #george #klaus #wilhelm #rebecca #2014 #pictures #sunset*.

The point behind this tagging convention is to make it easy to quickly find related notes in the future. In 2024, it will be easy to locate the right images if I want to find pictures of Klaus in Belmar.

Tagging Practice 7: Avoid Multiple-Word Tags

I feel multiple-word tags make it hard to find specific notes. When searching, you would have to remember that you used both words if you wanted to find anything. Trust me; this is hard to do *years after* creating a tag.

Let's give an example here. Instead of creating two tags with multiple words such as *"2013 ebooks"* and *"2014 ebooks,"* then I'd make sure to have a tag for every aspect of a note.

Example:

- 2014
- Ebooks
- Evernote

That way, if I want to find notes for all the books I publish in 2014, I'd a do a search like this: *tag:2014 tag:ebooks*. If I wanted to find the notes for *this* book, however, then I'd do this search: *tag:2014 tag:ebooks tag:evernote*.

Apply all seven of these practices to create a simple system for locating every note. You will be able to add thousands of notes in the next decade and never worry about losing an important idea.

And speaking of *how* to find things, the next section covers how to get the most from the search bar that comes standard with Evernote.

Evernote Basics: Making Evernote Search Work for You

One reason I spent so much time talking about tags and notebooks is because they become important while using *Evernote search*. Like Google and Yahoo, this app gives you the ability to search through mountains of content and quickly locate a specific item.

As we've discussed, when your notes start to number in the thousands, it'll be important to know have a system for finding everything. Here are seven tips to help you get started.

Tip #1: Understand the Basics of Evernote Search

Evernote works similarly to a search engine. Just find the search bar and start typing a word. The *difference* between the Evernote search function and a search engine is you'll often get more results than you actually need. And that's why I stress the importance of using multiple tags.

When starting a search, Evernote will pull words from tags, metadata, the content of each note and the OCR from pictures (more on this in a bit). The trick is to know *how* different types of search techniques will produce different results.

Here are a few examples and the results that they'd generate:

"potatoes"

- matches: "Four potatoes mashed together"
- doesn't match: "Sweet Potato Pie"

"Ever*" (A star at the end of a word will generate results for anything that includes the term or comes after the term in a block of text.)

- matches: "Evernote Corporation"
- does not match: "forevernote"

"San Francisco"

- matches: "San Francisco river valley"
- does not match: "San Marcos near the Francisco winery"

"ham"

- matches: "green eggs & ham."

"eggs ham"

- matches: "green eggs & ham."

When entering a search term, be aware of the naming and tagging conventions you've used in the past. And if you can't find a specific item? Try using different search qualifiers to see what comes up.

Tip #2: Don't Worry About Capitalization

Searches are *not* case sensitive, so it doesn't matter if you use capitals or not. Doing a search for "san francisco" will yield the same results as one for "*San Francisco*."

Tip #3: Save Your Searches

If you have a search you like, simply hit the "**+**" sign in the search box. This will save it for use in the future.

Tip #4: Search in Specific Notebooks

By default, searches are done across all notes and notebooks. That means if you type "Spanish" you will get results from your "Spanish Cooking" notebook in addition to notes from your "Spanish Language Lessons" notebook.

However if you do a search like this: **notebook:[nb name]** followed by the keyword, Evernote will only search in that notebook for the content.

For instance, if you wanted to find chicken recipes in your "Cooking" notebook, then you could do this search: **notebook:cooking chicken**.

Tip #5: Search by Tags

We've covered (ad nauseam) how tags make notes more searchable. By default, your tags will show up in search results in addition to other text and metadata. If a picture is tagged as "2014" with no other description or metadata, it will still be displayed in the results.

That said, there might be times when you want to do a search using just tags. Here are a few ways to do this:

- *Tag:[tag name]* will pull up every tag with that name.

- *Tag:[tag name*]* will generate tags that start with a specific string of text. This is useful if you ignored my earlier tips on tags and don't know if a specific tag uses a singular or plural version of a word.
- *-tag:[tag name]* will match any search term that **does not** have the chosen tag.

If you've established a large number of tags, you'll find that you can find pretty much anything with the search bar.

Tip #6: Search by Title

To be honest, I usually don't put a lot of thought into a note title. If your notes are very precise, however, you can easily find a specific item with this search string— *intitle:[search terms you desire]*. So a search for specific chicken recipes would become *intitle:chicken recipe*.

Tip #7: Search by Date

Perhaps you want to limit a search to a recent year or maybe you want to track down something you bookmarked a few years back. Regardless of the reason, it's easy to do a search in Evernote using dates.

The basic date search modifier works like this— *Created:[four-digit year+two-digit month+two-digit day]*. For instance, if you wanted to search all notes for the word "chicken," but only in entries after Feb 7, 2011, then your search modifier would be *chicken created:20110207*.

On the other hand, if you wanted to do a search of everything *before* that date, you'd simply add a negative modifier like—*chicken -created:20110207*.

We're almost at the end of the "basic" section, but before we jump into the advanced stuff, let's go over one last important principle of using Evernote.

Evernote Basics: Enhance Your Pictures Using OCR

A fun feature of Evernote is the ability to add and store *a lot* of pictures. More importantly, each image-based note instantly becomes searchable. When you send an image or screenshot to Evernote, their servers scan the note and pick out any words, labels or bits of handwriting displayed in the picture. Then they use this information to create an additional label for the picture.

In computer jargon, this feature is called "optical character recognition," or OCR for short. With OCR, you can create a fully searchable archive of every uploaded image, giving you a powerful tool for organizing your life.

Let me illustrate this feature with a specific example.

Imagine you're eating dinner in your favorite restaurant. On an impulse, you snap a photo of the menu and send it to Evernote. Later on, you're searching Evernote for "salmon" and suddenly this image pops up simply because the words "grilled salmon" were written on the menu. Or perhaps the restaurant names pops up when you're doing a related search. All of this happens *without* you adding tags or a description. Instead, it comes from the OCR picture of a menu. Cool, right?

OCR can be used on a variety of note types: warranties, gift cards, food labels, recipes and lists. It's the perfect archiving device for images that contain a lot of words. With a few taps of your smartphone, you can make the whole thing completely searchable.

The magic behind this process is a bit too technical for the scope of this book, but if you want to learn more about how it works, then I recommend reading this post on the Evernote blog: http://blog.evernote.com/tech/2013/07/18/how-evernotes-image-recognition-works/

We've now covered the basics of Evernote. To be honest, the previous chapters gave you just a glimpse of what you can accomplish with this program. Moving forward, we'll dive into the advanced features that will turn the boring "idea capture habit" into a life-changing habit that will impact everything you do on a daily basis.

Advanced Evernote: The Benefits of Importing Email

Creating content in Evernote is actually pretty self-explanatory. You type notes, record audio, and take pictures and save them all as notes. Then you place them into notebooks, insert a few tags and then move on. Easy, right?

To be honest, a number of competing apps have similar functions. Evernote *stands out* because it has advanced features that automate and systematize many of our day-to-day activities. Not only can you import email messages, audio files, PDFs and other documents, you can use Evernote as a central hub for managing your important files and pretty much everything else in your life.

One feature some people love is the ability to important email directly into Evernote. In many cases, this app serves as a better filing system than your email client does. In fact, a few people send *all* their emails to Evernote instead of using their email clients at all.

I'm not telling you to manage your inbox within Evernote, but if you want to do so, then there's a lot to learn about sending, filtering and forwarding emails. In this section, we'll briefly cover these concepts.

Why Send Emails to Evernote?

While you might not want to save every message, sending *some* to Evernote gives you a central location for storing receipts, travel information, purchase confirmations and other pieces of data that might be important in the future.

For instance, let's say you'd like to track your Amazon.com purchases. You could save the receipts in your email client, but when you have hundreds of similar messages, it's hard to find a receipt for a book you bought in 2012. By saving all of your Amazon receipts in Evernote, you can quickly find out which books you purchased in the past five years or even which ones relate to a favorite topic (fitness, productivity, etc.).

The email-to-Evernote process is something that many experienced users don't even think about, but it's actually pretty easy to set up.

How to Send Emails to Evernote

There are quite a few ways to send emails to Evernote, but let's take a look at the simplest method to see how you can quickly set up this filtering system.

Step 1: Find Your Unique Evernote Email ID.

When you sign up for Evernote, the company sends you a special email ID. It looks something like this: yourname.123abc@m.evernote.com.

Don't worry if you don't have this on hand. You can do the following to locate your specific ID number:

- Open the Evernote client
- Go to *Tools*
- Go to Account Info

- Copy the "email note to" link

Like I said, it's pretty straightforward.

Step 2: Add the Address to your Contact List

Create a new contact within your email client. Call it something clever (e.g. "Evernote"), then paste (or type in) the Evernote address.

At this point you have two choices: 1. Forward everything that interests you to Evernote, where the information is automatically added to a default notebook. 2. Follow the advanced strategy that's covered in the next few steps.

Step 3: Set Default Notebook (Optional)

As we discussed earlier, a default notebook starts off with a title such as *[your username] notebook,* but it is easy to change the notebook name to something else.

There are two ways to change a default notebook.

This is the first:

Evernote Client >> "Right-click" or "Tap" the notebook >> Properties >> Click the checkbox labeled "make this my default notebook".

The second method is for anyone who wants to keep the default folder as-is and use another one for email. To do this, you'll need to change the clip settings so emails are sent to an alternate folder.

Here's how to do this:

Evernote Client >> Tools >> Options >> Clipping >> Click the bubble "specify clip destination" >> Choose the folder you desire

Step 4: Use Tags and Other Identifiers (Optional)

If you're forwarding email on a message-by-message basis, there's no reason to set up an inbox or "pending" folder. That's because you have the ability to send email to any notebook, using tags and other identifiers within the message title.

This is a fairly simple process, but it might take a few tries before you remember the steps I'm about to detail:

- Send an email as I described in step #2.
- In the subject line, type in a title that describes the content.
- After the title, add an @ symbol followed by the name of the destination notebook. This will send the email it to that folder.
- After the @notebook, add specific tags (i.e. #kindle, #2014, #marketing).

Here's an example to explain this process.

When you bought this book, the wonderful folks at Amazon sent a receipt to your inbox. The subject line probably looks something like this: "Your Amazon Order #12345678910."

All you'd have to do is open the message and change the title to "Master Evernote @Amazon #ebooks #evernote #productivity #Evernote #2014." Then this email would be sent to an "Amazon" notebook along with the tags *ebooks, evernote, 2014* and *productivity*. This is assuming that you set up this notebook and set of tags ahead of time.

The best part? It won't be hard to find this receipt in the future if you search for the order number or use search phrases such as *productivity*, *ebooks*, and *2014*.

This is a simple way to archive a message on a case-by-case, but as I mentioned before, some people prefer Evernote to their standard email clients. In the next section, I'll briefly describe how to automate the delivery of email to your Evernote account.

Advanced Evernote: How to

Automate Your Email Delivery

Perhaps you want to respond to all email messages via Evernote. The truth is Evernote *can* do this, but there is a specific process for setting it up.

To start, you should know that each email client works differently. In this section, we'll talk about Outlook, since it's the program many people use. That said, you can easily find a tutorial for any email client using this phrase: *[your email client] email forwarding*. If you use Gmail, then you'd enter *Gmail email forwarding*.

Here's how to forward a message using Outlook:

Click the "gear" symbol >> Options >> Email Forwarding >> Select the "Forward your mail to another email account" radio button >> Insert your Evernote email address (the address you created in step #1 of sending emails) >> Click the "Save" button.

Sound too complicated?

If so, here's a screenshot of all three screens to show this works:

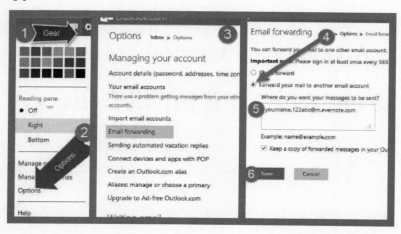

To be honest, I don't sort email with Evernote (my preference is to manage everything with Gmail), so I suggest you check out the "Evernote Scott" YouTube channel that provides a wealth of in-depth information on this subject.

The playlist found here: http://bit.ly/1xvVfxX includes a number of advanced tutorials. If you want to integrate your email and contacts, check out videos six through nine as well as video #18.

Advanced Evernote: Scan
Documents Using CamScanner

S canning documents directly to your computer is an
  important part of creating a paperless lifestyle. The best
    part? When you uploaded digitized files to Evernote,
you make each note fully searchable with the OCR feature.

Many scanners work well with Evernote. Instead of
boring you with a laundry list of options, I will keep things
simple by recommending an app called <u>CamScanner</u>.

CamScanner is simply one of the best tools I've found
for digitizing any file. It uses the camera on your mobile
device to scan any document. To instantly scan a
document, simply download the app, turn it on and use a
smooth motion to pass your mobile device over the
document you want to scan.

In my opinion, the most important feature of
CamScanner is it works seamlessly with Evernote. You can
quickly digitize a document, add it to Evernote and then
use its OCR feature to collect data for a future search.

CamScanner is just one of the many apps that I
recommend. We'll talk about more other available apps
near the end of this book.

Advanced Evernote: Create IFTTT Recipes for Evernote

IFTTT.com stands for *If This, Then That*. IFTTT is a website *and* app that automates processes between two different services. So when "Action X" is completed on the first service, "Action Y" will happen. That's why it's cleverly named *If This, Then That*.

Note: IFTT doesn't work with some browsers. If you have trouble accessing this site, then try switching to a different browser. My recommendation is Firefox.

IFTTT runs on what they call "recipes." Anyone can build recipes for their favorite programs or apps, but there are more than 8,400 recipes specifically for Evernote as of July 2014. Visit https://ifttt.com/evernote to browse through all of them.

To get started, check out recipes that will help you increase your productivity and organize your personal life:

- Amazon Receipts to Evernote
- Automatically back up Tweets to Evernote.
- Download Instagram photos I like to Evernote.
- Star an item in Gmail. It is automatically sent to Evernote.

- Star something in Pocket. It is automatically sent to Evernote.
- Archive Instagram photos.
- Connect Google Talk or Siri to Evernote.
- Save Facebook status updates in running timelines.
- RSS Feeds to Evernote
- Google Calendar to-do lists sent to/updated by Evernote
- Archive all Foursquare check-ins in a single note.
- Get a list of new books for your Kindle to Evernote.
- New Dropbox files are copied to Evernote.

This list should spark a few ideas. All you have to do is use the search bar on IFTTT to find what's available. If you want to automate processes between Evernote and Siri, simply search for *Evernote Siri* to find available recipes.

If you get nothing else from this book, hopefully you'll learn that IFTTT provides a treasure trove of ideas for using Evernote to save time and organize your life.

Since this isn't a book on IFTTT, I'll simply say it's worthwhile to set aside a few hours to think about the time-consuming activities you do on specific websites or apps. Write them down on a piece of paper. Then go search for each one on IFTTT and see if there's a recipe that automates this process. Odds are, you can easily save an hour or so every week with this simple exercise.

Advanced Evernote: Use Web Clipper to Bookmark Important Sites

Evernote Web Clipper (http://evernote.com/webclipper/) is an add-on for a number of browsers (Firefox, Chrome, Safari, Opera and Internet Explorer). It's packaged separately since it's uploaded directly to your preferred browser. The reason I recommend this tool is because it can import all sorts of text, data, pictures and files directly to Evernote.

What Does Web Clipper Do?

Here are some of the things you can do with Web Clipper:

- Clip parts of an article for later use.
- Collect entire articles to be read later.
- Save content or pictures, then mark them up to share your thoughts with others.
- Build a database of "tickler files" and future ideas.

In essence, what Web Clipper gives you is a simple tool for bookmarking any site on your desktop and saving the information within Evernote. Whenever you find a page worth remembering, you can quickly add it to Evernote with this extension.

How to Capture a Web Clip

The picture below shows you everything you need to know for clipping a page. This is a Firefox screenshot, but your browser should a have a fairly similar look:

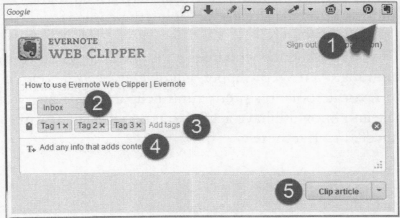

Let's go over each step of the process:

1.   Click the "Elephant" icon on your browser toolbar to pull up Web Clipper.

2.   Pick the notebook where you'd like to save the clip. By default, I have mine set to "Inbox" because I tag and change notebooks in bulk later in the week. It is easy to change notebooks while you clip websites, so don't feel like you have to use the same notebook every time.

3.   Insert tags to match the Web clipping.

4.   Add text that describes the article and why it's being clipped. This creates context and helps you figure out the clip's importance in the future.

5.   Pick one of three options. 1. Clip the article to grab just the center content and eliminate the sidebar junk and advertisements. 2. Clip the entire page to save everything on your screen. 3. Clip URL to copy the address of the page without saving the content.

If you're someone who does a lot of desktop and laptop computing, then Web Clipper will quickly become one of your favorite tools. It's pretty fun to clip a compelling article and know I'll have access to it on every platform connected to Evernote.

Advanced Evernote: Importing Folders to Evernote

Another advanced strategy is importing folders and saving them to Evernote's cloud servers. This hack is useful if you're worried about losing important documents or prefer the security of having a perpetual backup. For example, if you write a lot and want to make sure every piece of content is saved somewhere other than your computer hard drive, this is a great option.

Importing folders doesn't require an all-or-nothing approach. Simply set up your computer to monitor a *specific* folder and copy the content to Evernote whenever you add a new file or update an existing file. Then later on, you move around the individual files, adding tags and specific descriptions.

Here's a personal example. As you can probably guess, I do a lot of writing. Blog posts, ebooks, emails and personal journal entries are all an important part of my life and business. So whenever I write, it's comforting to know the content is backed up on Evernote's servers.

How to Create an Import Folder

Unfortunately, at the time of this writing, the *import folders* feature is only available in the Windows version (http://evernote.com/evernote/guide/windows/) of Evernote. If this is the version you use, here's how to set it up:

1. Create a new folder or choose an existing folder to import. You should be comfortable with this information being stored in cloud server. If a certain file contains sensitive information (such as a password), then think twice about automatically backing it up.

2. Use a folder name that's easy to identify. Being the clever guy that I am, mine is called: "Evernote import folder."

3. Go to the Evernote for Windows program. Choose *Tools >> Import Folders >>* Click *Add*.

4. Add any folder that you want to import. The trick here is to include each sub-folder because they're not automatically imported. This is easy to do. Simply click the "yes" checkbox for adding subfolders and everything will be ready to go.

5. Evernote will keep the original files in your folder, plus it copies them to their servers. If you want to remove a file after it has been added, simply click the dropdown menu and select the *Delete* button.

You don't have to import *every* folder, but it's a good idea if you constantly travel or work exclusively with a laptop. You never know when a computer will be stolen or damaged. By automatically backing up your files to Evernote, you'll have the peace of mind of knowing the important stuff is stored in a safe, secure location.

Advanced Evernote: Mark Up Photos and Images with Skitch

Skitch is another free add-on that lets you "mark up" screenshots, graphics and photos. You either grab an existing image *or* take a photo (with your mobile device). Then you add simple graphics to help explain a concept to others.

These are just some of the features available in Skitch:

- Circles
- Arrows
- Ellipses
- Rectangles
- Rounded Rectangles
- Pixilation
- Highlighter
- Marker
- Textetti
- Mouse entry
- Lines
- Crop

- Resize

As an example, here is a screenshot from my blog, DevelopGoodHabits.com. I used Skitch to mark up the screenshot with circles, arrows and other embellishments. Here's how it looks:

Notice how the arrows and circles point out different sections of the website? That's the purpose of Skitch—it makes it easy to explain something by taking a quick picture and marking it up with text or graphics.

That's just a basic overview of this tool, so let's talk about how to use it to organize your life.

10 Ways to Use Skitch

1. **Collaborate with Others.** When working with others, a marked-up picture sometimes gets the point across better than your words. What you get with Skitch

is an intuitive graphics program that lets you share images and *show* something instead of trying to write it down.

2. **Resize Images.** With Skitch, you get an easy interface for resizing images. Open an existing image (or take a new screenshot), then drag from the bottom right corner to get the border you want. Select "Save" and you have a new resized image.

3. **Crop Images.** In Skitch, cropping works the same way as resizing an image.

4. **Save to Evernote**. Skitch has a large "Save to Evernote" button designed to work with seamlessly with Evernote as a core function. Other graphics programs don't have this capability.

5. **Add Text.** A popular use of Skitch is adding text to an image. Use this feature to add quotes, important information or notes to yourself.

6. **Insert Graphics.** Another way to use Skitch as a collaborative tool is to take an image and insert markup graphics (like arrows, circles and lines) to demonstrate a concept you're trying to explain.

7. **Share with Others.** Skitch offers a simple interface for sharing images on social media sites such as Facebook, LinkedIn and Twitter.

8. **Use Webcam Shots.** Skitch also works well with your webcam. Use it the same way you would any other

image application—take a photo, load it in Skitch and then use markup to add your thoughts.

9. **Save Images in a Variety of Formats.** Skitch makes it easy to save and export your pictures in a variety of formats (.jpg, .png, .tif and .svg).

10. **Turn Files Into PDFs.** Skitch also allows you to turn any file into a PDF without having to download Adobe Acrobat. This is a great way to ensure other people will be able to open the files you share.

While Skitch isn't as robust as other graphics programs, it's handy for adding your ideas to images and then sharing those images with others.

That concludes our discussion of the advanced features of Evernote. The final section of this book will show you how to use Evernote to organize your entire life. With the tips and tricks featured in the next section, you'll save time, reduce paper clutter and increase your productivity.

So far, I've only *hinted* at what Evernote can do. This app actually makes it possible to keep track of important projects and get more done in less time, so let's take a look at how to use it with a wildly popular productivity system.

How to Organize Your Life – the
Getting Things Done System

Let me start with a brief disclaimer. In the next few sections, we'll talk heavily about applying David Allen's *Getting Things Done* (GTD) system with the Evernote app. The following is designed to increase your productivity and improve your time management skills, but this method is *not* for everyone because it requires a high level of commitment to the process.

So if you're happy with your current level of productivity, then you have my permission to skip ahead to the section where we talk about 75 ideas for getting started with Evernote.

What is GTD?

The purpose of GTD is to take ideas, tasks and projects out of your mind and create a series of actionable tasks. The idea here is to stop *thinking* about what you need to do and start focusing on actually getting things done. While I don't agree with *everything* Allen teaches, I feel GTD provides a great framework for being productive on a day-to-day basis.

The main purpose of GTD is simple: **Clearing the mind creates a constant efficient and productive state.**

It all boils down to focus.

Normal productivity is stymied by lack of focus. Even if you have a perfect working environment without any external interruptions, your mind often betrays you.

For instance, you might start working on a task (like writing an article) and have other thoughts pop up in your mind (e.g. "Did I send a response to that customer's email?"). Then you check your inbox and see a reminder of yet another action you didn't start yet (such as booking reservations for your upcoming vacation). Then your thoughts suddenly spiral out of control: "I forgot about my dental appointment!" "My wife keeps reminding me about the home repairs." "Why do I always feel buried under the things I have to do?"

These thoughts often plague your subconscious mind (or even your conscious mind) because of something called an "open loop."

Think of it this way. I'm sure you've heard a song on the radio and had it end halfway through. What usually happens then? Often the song will keep popping into your mind, again and again. This is an open loop because your mind never experienced the *closure* of hearing the song end.

Incomplete tasks work the same way. When your mind feels like something hasn't been completed, it will continue to expend "mental RAM" thinking about it in the background.

Ultimately, what Allen tries to teach is a "mind like water" approach to productivity.

In Getting Things Done, he puts it best:

"Imagine throwing a pebble into a pond. How does the water respond? The answer is, totally appropriately to the force and mass of the input, then it returns to calm. It doesn't overreact or underreact."

This is the "purpose" of GTD. It's a system that allows you to react with just the right level of response. When you adopt his strategy, you'll learn how to prioritize tasks properly, organize your workflow and deal with specific tasks in the appropriate manner.

So how does GTD actually work?

In the next section, we'll go over its five basic steps.

Five Basic Steps of Getting Things Done

Now let's talk about the specifics of GTD. To start, below is a basic flowchart of the GTD process, with my own modifications of how to use it conjunction with Evernote. (You can also see a large version of this chart here: http://www.developgoodhabits.com/gtd-flowchart.jpg)

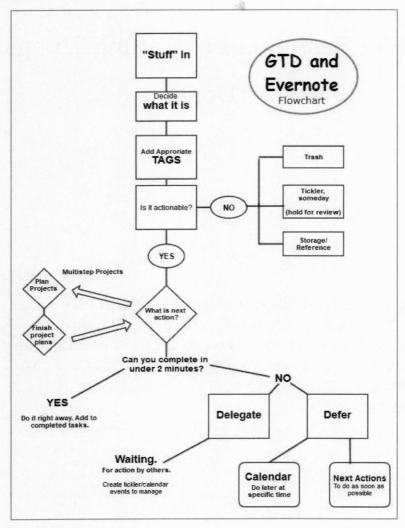

The process, really, is broken down into five basic steps:

1. Collection
2. Process
3. Organization
4. Review
5. Do

Here is an explanation of how each works:

#1. Collection: This is all the "stuff" that goes into Evernote: personal and professional paperwork, health documents, emails, photos, projects and simple reminders.

When it comes to Evernote, pretty much *anything* can be included in this first step.

So if you wonder, "Is this really worth putting into Evernote?" the answer is YES. During the processing stage, you can always choose to delete a note, but it's often impossible to add something later if you never took the time to initially write it down.

#2. Process: This is the important step of taking the "inbox" and making it "empty," so you need to complete this step on a regular basis. In fact, turn it into a habit. For instance, I like to empty my Evernote inbox every Sunday during a weekly review session.

#3. Organization: Like Evernote, the key to using GTD effectively is being organized. This means having a system in place so you know where to find everything and what projects require your immediate attention.

The basic organization of GTD follows the Evernote flowchart from before. We'll go over it in more detail and talk about how to build a good system using Evernote.

#4. Review: Monitoring your system regularly ensures it doesn't break down. This is means doing more than clearing the inbox. It means looking at your calendar, project lists, single tasks and long-term goals.

A good review is also the time to add miscellaneous items that haven't been organized and perform the tasks necessary for getting all of your important information in one place. Here are some ideas:

- Gathering loose notes
- Scanning in articles that interest you

- Putting ideas into the "note" format
- Review project lists and action lists
- Reviewing someday/maybe files
- Reviewing "pending" files
- Reviewing your calendar

Again, I recommend turning this into a weekly habit. Try to do it at the end of the week (sometime between Friday and Sunday) so you end the week on a good note and have a chance to prepare for the next one.

#5. Do: This is where you actually *get things done*. The first tasks to complete are the items in the "next actions" file.

After that, work on tasks based on the context you've previously assigned each one. If several tasks have the tag "phone calls," set aside a block of time to complete all of these tasks.

The context of a task is based on four categories:

1. *Context.* As mentioned earlier, this refers to grouping similar items together and working on them as a group. An example would be completing a series of scheduled phone calls.

2. *Time Available.* If you only have 15 minutes free for a task, it is best to work on a task that will take that amount of time. You should only work on longer tasks when you have time to give them your full attention.

3. *Energy Available.* For some tasks, you might need an energy "boost" before starting. There are other tasks you shouldn't attempt unless you are at your peak. For me, this is my writing. I write first thing in the morning because I am at my freshest and best. When you know a

task is tough, be sure to routinely schedule it when you are at your best.

4. *Priority.* This is an obvious one. If task A has a greater priority to you, do it before task B.

When deciding which tasks to complete, use the criteria above to determine which task to tackle first. If you only have a few minutes in between meetings, pick a task that will only take a minute or two. Save complicated tasks for when you have the time to focus on them.

That was a very brief overview of *Getting Things Done*. Now let's talk about how to use Evernote to assist you with these activities.

GTD + Evernote: Three Basic Requirements

It doesn't take much to follow the GTD strategy with Evernote, but you do need three things to be successful.

#1. Time

In the long run, this process will save you massive amounts of time, but before that happens, you'll need to make some time commitments.

First you have to digitize all the "stuff" that's important in your life and add it to Evernote. Next, you will need to set aside a specific amount of time each week to manage your "inbox". Finally, you have to commit to the entire process, not just the items that seem interesting.

#2. Space

Using Evernote with GTD eliminates a lot of space requirements (like the need for a filing cabinet and piles of folders) because everything will be stored in a digital version. That said, it's still important to have space where you can do work.

This work area should be your command center. A functional, clean and clear workspace mirrors a functional, clean and clear mind, which is the ultimate goal of "getting things done."

#3. Tools

One of the big differences between "classic GTD" and "Evernote GTD" are the tools involved. In his book, David Allen recommends a number of tools:

- Paper holding trays
- Paperclips
- Binding clips
- Stapler
- Rubber bands
- Tape
- Calendar
- File folders
- File cabinets
- Labeler
- Pen/pencil

As you can see, these tools may be essential for "real-world" application of GTD, but you don't need any of them if you use Evernote for GTD. The purpose of each item is processing massive amounts of paperwork, but since you're putting most items into Evernote, you don't need to worry that much about a paper-based workflow.

How to Set Up a GTD and Evernote Process Flow

Now it's time to explain how this all works. The core purpose of Evernote is to store and manage all the "stuff" in your life, so the rest of this section will describe the process of putting random items in Evernote and adding them to your GTD process.

To start, look again at the diagram from before.

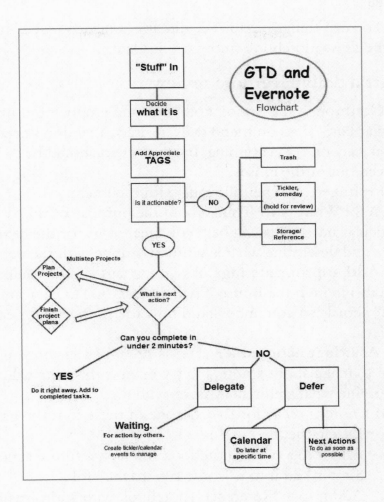

Let's go over each step of this process.

Stuff in

This includes pretty much every note you will add to Evernote: emails, ideas, scanned documents, photos and project lists. The idea here is to use the app for pure data collection. If you know where a note goes, then place it in the appropriate notebook. If you don't have a particular notebook in mind, you should still add the information to Evernote and sort it later.

To keep things organized, add any "uncategorized" note to the *!Inbox* notebook (more on this later).

Start a daily Evernote review

Go through the !Inbox notebook and empty it out on a regular basis (I recommend daily at first). You don't need to take action on everything, but each item should be moved out of the inbox.

From here, do the following with each item:

#1. Ask: What is it? Think about the purpose of this particular note. This will help you create tags for the next stage and determine what is ultimately done with the item.

#2. Add appropriate tags. Assigning tags is how you'll find this item in the future. I will discuss "GTD navigation tags" shortly so you understand how to set up tags for easy retrieval.

#3. Ask: Is it actionable? This is first big decision you have to make about a note. How you view this note will determine what's ultimately done with it.

If a note is *not* actionable, do one of these four things:

1. Delete the file.
2. Add it to a tickler notebook for *possible* future action.
3. Simply add it to a "someday/maybe" folder.
4. Add it to a "Reference" notebook with appropriate tags for future retrieval.

If it is actionable, you have to make your next big decision: *What action needs to be taken?*

#4. Decide on the next action. This step requires more thought than you might realize.

"Finish budget," for example, is not a good next action because you might need a specific piece of information to get started. A better step would be to "Call Bob about his budget numbers."

#5. Create a project list: Multi-step projects don't always have a clear-cut "next action" from the very beginning. You need to create a plan and then develop a list of tasks to incorporate into your workflow.

#6. Ask: Does the action take less than two minutes? Two minutes is an arbitrary time that Allen says should be used to take immediate action on items. The idea is that if a task can be completed in this short amount of time, you should immediately handle it. If a task *might* turn into a longer task, however, then you need to process it with the rest of the steps.

So:

Tasks < 2 Minutes = Do it

Tasks > 2 Minutes = Defer/Delegate it

#7: Delegate appropriate tasks. This is where the next step (or entire project) is completed by someone else. It's important to *not* send this task out into the void and *assume* it will be handled. When delegating a task, the recipient should be clear about the expectations and understand *when* you expect results.

A great way to follow up on a delegated task is to use the calendars and alarms that come with Evernote. Pick a date for when the task should be completed and then set up a reminder.

#8: Defer everything else. If a note isn't immediately actionable, but might be someday, then you want to do one of two things:

(I). Create a calendar event. If you don't want to deal with an item today, but you might want to do it in the future, create an Evernote reminder to follow up on it.

This step is an important one. Remember how we talked earlier about how the subconscious can "worry" about uncompleted tasks, killing your productivity? A simple way to eliminate this anxiety is to "know" you'll take care of it sometime in the future.

(II). Add it to next actions. Instead of completely deferring a project, you could add the first action to the "next actions" note. These actions are to be completed as soon as possible and should be based on your priorities, time available, energy and any "grouping" of similar tasks.

That's a simple overview of the GTD process. Now let's talk about how to create an Evernote-specific version of this productivity method.

How to Set Up GTD Notebooks

In the first part of this book, we talked about setting up notebooks. The process works similarly with GTD, but my advice is to keep things simple and use a minimum amount of notebooks. Think of them as your inbox, outbox and storage areas. As Allen once said, the goal is to have *"as many as you need, but as few as you can get away with."*

To get started, I recommend creating a stack called "GTD" or something along those lines. From there, create three to four notebooks, which should help keep this area free of clutter.

1: !Inbox

This is the dumping ground where you send emails, uncategorized notes, scanned items and every random thought you record.

As I discussed earlier, a core philosophy of GTD is taking the time to decide if something is actionable. Then you should do it, delegate it, defer it, delete it or delay it.

The main difference between a GTD inbox and an Evernote inbox is that you sort GTD items based on specific decisions. You will have to work your way through the GTD process flow and determine the best way to handle a particular task.

After running a note through the GTD process flow, you have three choices:

1. Delete the note.
2. Tag it and send it to a "completed" notebook.
3. Tag it and send it to a "storage" notebook.

Let's talk about these other items.

2: Completed

Once items have been tagged *and* you've taken the appropriate action, you can add them to this notebook.

3: Storage/Reference

As you know, space isn't an issue with Evernote. Some notes may never be used again, but you should consider storing them on the off chance they might be needed.

4: Shared Tasks/Delegated

This final notebook is completely optional. If you work with teams or often share information with others, then they should be included in this section. This is the notebook you'll share with others.

In all other notebooks, I stress economy when it comes to GTD. Why clutter things up when you're trying to be organized? However, with this option, you might want to create separate notebooks based on the nature of the relationship you have with each recipient.

Some people might be partners in your business, so they should have full access to all your files. Those who have small roles in your business should have limited access to your files. My advice is to create separate notebooks and think carefully about *what* documents are stored in each area.

Like everything else with Evernote, you get the best results by using an organized *tagging* system, so let's talk about how to set that up.

How to Set Up Tags for GTD

When you set up Evernote with a specific organizational goal in mind, the heavy lifting is done by tags because (as we've discussed) there's no limit to the number of tags you can create.

The trick here is to set up your tags in a way that they work in conjunction with GTD.

For instance, you have a bunch of options with a note that's sitting in your inbox:

- Do it (if less than 2 minutes).
- Assign it to a project.
- Trash it.
- Defer it to your someday/maybe notebook.
- Add it to a reference notebook.
- Delegate the task to others.
- Label it a "Next Action" to be completed with batched tasks.
- Create/schedule a calendar event

The question is: *What's the best way to use tags with the GTD system?*

The short answer is to use **navigational tags**.

These tags are not actually used on any active notes. They're designed help you find other tags. In other words, they provide a navigational aid, just like the name suggests.

Here is an example of what I am talking about:

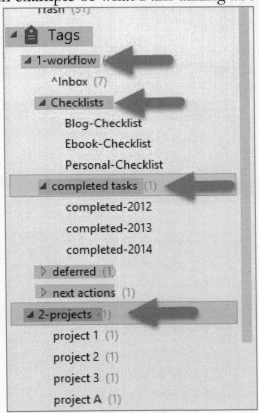

Notice how all navigational tags include a triangle next to them? This shows that there are *additional* tags underneath them. This is why tags work well with GTD: you set up the navigation one time and then you can use this system to quickly filter each future note.

Creating a navigational tag setup isn't hard. Create the tags you desire, then drag them over the tag that will act as the main tag. Evernote will then nest the navigational tags underneath the main tag.

For instance, let's say you have a tag called "projects" and a series of projects with tags such as "project 1," "project 2" and "project 3." All you have to do is drag each over the projects tag and Evernote will put them underneath this tag.

To further elaborate on this idea, let's take a look at what could happen when you're processing a brand new note using the Evernote/GTD system.

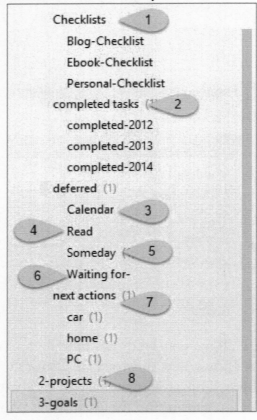

The picture above shows that there is a very limited number of actions to take with any new note that's filtered through the GTD system.

1. Add it to a checklist for later action.

2. Do it now! (If it will take less than two minutes, take action and immediately add it to your list of completed tasks.)

3. Create a calendar event for the task.

4. Create a task to read/ research and gather more information.

5. Add the task to the "someday/maybe" file of things you might pursue in the future.

6. Add the note here if you're waiting for something before taking action.

7. Set the task for a "next action" and sub-divide it according to where you will complete the work (i.e. car, phone or computer).

8. Set the task if it's part of a larger ongoing project.

As you can see, it's not hard to set up navigational tags. With this simple system, you can use tags to help you create action-based notes and easily find them in the future.

Final Thoughts on Using GTD with Evernote

This section gave you a few basic pointers on using *Getting Things Done* with the Evernote app. To be honest, this is just the tip of iceberg. My recommendation? Take some time to read (or re-read) this guide to see how it will improve your productivity. Then take each part of Allen's system and look for ways to use it with Evernote.

Now, GTD is just *one* use for this app. In fact, there is so much more you can do with it on a daily basis. In the next section, we'll cover 75 different ideas for getting the most out of Evernote.

75 Ideas for Getting Started with Evernote

Up to this point, we've primarily talked about how Evernote is a great productivity tool. Odds are that's probably why *you* initially wanted to check it out. The truth is, getting things done is only the tip of the iceberg when it comes to using Evernote.

The beauty of Evernote goes beyond "what it can do." It's actually not that hard to set up notes, tags, notebooks and stacks. What makes this tool great is the **mindset** you will develop as you use it to organize your life.

In this section, I give you 75 ideas for getting started with Evernote. Honestly, *this* is the fun stuff. It doesn't matter if you're a student, employee, parent, business owner or productivity enthusiast; you will find something useful here.

Let's get to it.

Ideas #1: Go Paperless

When you upload documents, ideas, receipts, statements, to-do lists and all the rest of your files to Evernote, you decrease paper clutter. This is the first step toward having a single place to keep all your paperwork. All you have to do then is sign up for digital copies of your bills and you'll be well on your way to living a paperless existence.

Honestly, "physical copies" of documents are quickly becoming outdated. If you have a good system for scanning documents, creating backups and using tags, you'll find it's no longer necessary to keep that "box full of receipts" like you once did.

Ideas #2: Review Educational Information

It doesn't matter if you're no longer in school. At some point, you'll probably take notes while reading a nonfiction book or learning a new skill. The trick is to have constant access to these notes instead of jotting them down on the yellow legal pad that gets lost in the pile of clutter on your desk.

Reviewing educational information with Evernote isn't hard. Simply type (or copy and paste) each lesson into a file and attach it to a note. As with other aspects of Evernote, the key is to use a good naming convention for titles, notebooks and tags. That way, you can quickly find every lesson you've ever recorded.

Idea #3: Organize Notes/Bookmarks into a Virtual Learning System

If you want to research a new topic or learn a skill, you will need information from a variety of sources. In other words, you learn best when you do a "deep dive" on a subject and locate a variety of useful websites, courses, books and tools. Information from each source should end up as a separate note.

With Evernote, you can group these notes together in a notebook and create your own virtual classroom.

EXAMPLE:

In the last few weeks, I've explored the idea of integrating Instagram with my Kindle business. So during the past week, I've added notes, explored ideas and bookmarked Instagram-specific websites. Some of these thoughts might not pan out, but at this point, I now have a large collection of strategies I could implement with this app.

Idea #4: Add Personal Thoughts to Your Web Clips

I read many great articles, but there are times I only need to remember a short passage. With Skitch, I can easily clip sections of a post and mark it up with my thoughts. This makes it easy to save important pieces of content without being forced to read an entire article and try to remember *why* I added it to Evernote.

Whenever I find a good article on Instagram, for example, I only clip the sections containing *actionable* pieces of information. In the future, I won't have to waste time reading through a lengthy preamble on *why* Instagram is important when all I want to do is review the actionable content.

Idea #5: Record Ideas on the Fly

I have always been obsessed with taking notes. Once upon a time, I jotted ideas down on scraps of paper I quickly misplaced. After that, it was a small "idea notebook" that I would often forget to bring with me. Now with Evernote, I finally have a central location for storing every good idea.

What I like about Evernote is you never have to worry about "where" to save everything. You write down a thought, tag it with the right label and upload it to the app. Then every week or so, you can go into Evernote and organize the ideas you've added during the previous seven days.

Idea #6 Take Photo Notes

They say a picture is worth a thousand words. Instead of trying to explain a specific problem, it's often easier to snap a photo and mark it up with arrows and circles.

The other day, I was talking to my landlord about a leaky roof. Instead of trying to explain the problem, I took a few pictures, added markup graphics and sent the image as a text message.

Sometimes you don't even need to add text to a note. See something you want to buy? Feel inspired by a piece of art? Want to document damage to your vehicle? Simply snap a photo, save it in Evernote and use it to jog your memory at another time.

Idea #7: Create "Word-to-Text" Notes

For hyper-productive people, *writing down* a note takes too much time. This is when the "word-to-text" feature that comes standard with most smartphones comes in handy. Simply create a reminder by speaking into your phone and using the word-to-text feature.

With tweaking through IFTTT.com, you don't even have to open Evernote to create a note. Once you create a recipe, everything you say to Siri or Google Talk will automatically be sent to Evernote (here's a great IFTTT recipe for getting started).

Idea #8: Record Regular Audio Notes

Some people prefer recording audio notes instead of using the word-to-text feature because voice recognition software doesn't always get the words right. This is a useful feature because you will be able to review your audio notes during your weekly review session.

Idea #9: Use Penultimate to Sketch Out Ideas

Penultimate is an app that gives you a blank canvas with an assortment of drawing and writing tools. With this tool, Evernote becomes a personal sketch page for mapping out thoughts or processes.

Like other add-ons, it's not as robust as a full graphics program, but it's useful for those times when you want to think things out on paper.

Idea #10: Collect Social Media Updates

You probably think of great things all day long: a good joke, a news item, a pithy comment or an inspiring idea. The problem? Sometimes it's not the right moment to share it with the rest of the world via social media.

With Evernote, however, you can quickly turn into the funniest, most insightful person in your social media circle. Simply create a notebook titled "Social Media" (or Twitter, Facebook or Instagram if you prefer). Then use this notebook to collect all the funny and interesting observations you make throughout the day. Once you have time to post to your social media account, go through the notebook until you find just the right thought for the occasion.

Idea #11: Work on That Next Piece of Poetry (or Music)

Truth be told, I'm not very artistic. That said, I'm friends with a few writers and artists who swear by the power of using Evernote to record ideas for their next pieces. With this tool you can record abstract thoughts and use your subconscious mind to work out all the details. In a way, this is similar to brainstorming every element of a project.

Idea #12: Create Extensive Outlines

Outlining isn't something you just do in school. In fact, any creative project could benefit from doing an extensive outline. Every time you start a new project, create a new notebook for your ideas. Use this notebook to store project-related links, tools and thoughts. The more you add to this notebook, the better the outcome of your project.

As an example, this book (and pretty much every Kindle book I've written) starts out in Evernote. Whenever I get a book idea, I create a notebook and add notes for several weeks before I start writing. I use these notes to create a simple outline of my ideas, which ultimately becomes my first draft.

Idea #13: Share Work with Others [Premium Feature]

If you and your team members are *premium* Evernote customers, then you can access the same notes and make instant changes. As an added bonus, these changes are immediately accessible to everyone else on your team. This is what makes Evernote such an exceptional collaborative tool.

Idea #14: Build a Digital "Filing Cabinet" for School

If you're still in school, Evernote can become a digital dumping ground for everything you've accomplished. Keep copies of all papers and reports. Take pictures of all tests, quizzes and class assignments and save each as a note. By doing this, you can keep a record of everything you've done throughout the course of your school career.

Idea #15: Keep Notes for Every Class

On a more granular level, you can use Evernote like a notebook. Simply use a tool like CamScanner to take pictures and digitize each lesson. This will give you a nice chronological study guide that can be accessed on every device that's connected to your Evernote account.

You can even take pictures of important class handouts and practice tests, which is something you can't do with paper notebooks.

Idea #16: Record Classes

Take audio notes and record your classes. You can then use a "word-to-text" recipe to create an automatic transcription, listen to the lesson again or take notes as an additional way to remember the content.

Idea #17: Digitize Your Textbooks

Instead of lugging around six textbooks, you can take pictures of what you need to study and have it accessible on your mobile device. This works similar to the three previous ideas. By uploading the content to class-specific notebooks, it will be ready to study wherever you go.

Idea #18: Collect PDF Versions of Your Syllabi

The syllabus for each of your classes clearly spells out what you need to do to get a good grade. My advice is to upload each syllabus and add it to a class-specific notebook. As you're studying, you'll have a constant reminder of what elements a particular teacher thinks are important.

Idea #19: Handwritten School Notes.

Some students prefer to write their notes by hand instead of using a laptop. You can instantly digitize these notes with a few different options.

First, the Penultimate app allows you to draw pictures using the canvas feature. This a great option if a specific class includes a lot of diagrams.

You can also type out the class material and attach it to a note.

Finally, you can write out notes the old-fashioned way (pen and paper) and take a picture with CamScanner.

Idea #20: Maintain Your Important Information

It's hard to remember every possible piece of information: passcodes, website logins, lock combos, account numbers and important phone numbers. Evernote makes it possible to create a database for storing everything in a central location.

Obviously, this idea is completely optional. Some people are uncomfortable with the idea of storing sensitive information in a digital format. My advice is to use some discretion here. Either use an additional password with this file or don't include any piece of data that can be used for identity theft (such as your Social Security number).

Idea #21: Map Out Project Lists

Creating actionable lists is the key to completing any project. Each list item should be a specific task with a measurable outcome. For example, "Lose five pounds by July 30" is better than "lose weight" because it is more specific.

With Evernote, you can create a note for each project and use a checkbox to-do list. As you complete one task, look at the following item on the list to see what you need to do next. Add these project lists to a notebook titled "Action Folder," and you'll have a central location for the tasks you need to complete in the near future.

Idea #22: Create a Weekly Action List

A weekly action list takes the concept of the project list one step further. At the start of the week (I prefer Sundays), go through each of your project lists and identify the most important items for your personal and professional life. Instead of having to rely on multiple project lists, you'll have a small collection of tasks that will be the focus for the next seven days.

Get started by creating a simple checklist within a note. Put this note in a notebook called "!Weekly" so it shows up near the top of your Evernote dashboard. Then open this list on a daily basis to see what tasks you need to complete.

Idea #23: Create Process Checklists

Process checklists are a little different than project lists because they describe the step-by-step actions of a regular process. The benefit of writing everything down is you either identify ways to improve the process *or* train someone else to handle this task.

Using a previous example, I follow a 34-step process list for publishing a new Kindle book. The process checklist helps me identify the tasks I complete on my own (i.e. writing the book, creating marketing material and crafting the promotional email) versus what can be delegated to a team member (i.e. graphics, edits and routine marketing).

Idea #24: Organize Your Research

Whether you're in school or own your own business, it's important to make research and continued self-education an important part of your day. The good news? Evernote makes it easy to put every link, chart, PDF, article and excerpt into a central location that's easy to search on multiple devices.

Overall, this tool is a big improvement over the browser full of bookmarks you thought were important. This also beats the pants off of frantically searching your hard drive and Web history for sources when a due date is looming.

Idea #25: Record Business Meetings

Make audio recordings of important meetings and save them to Evernote. This frees you up your time so you never miss an important task. You can also have these notes transcribed or use them to assign projects to specific members of your team.

This idea can also minimize future legal problems. For instance, if you operate an LLC with another person, it's important to keep minutes of each meeting because it shows you're functioning as a legitimate business instead of as a personal entity. This can be important if you ever get sued and a lawyer is trying to go after your personal assets.

Idea #26: Download Product Manuals

All products come with an owner's manual. These items aren't immediately important, but *might be* sometime in the future, so you're afraid to throw them out.

What you might not know is most products have a PDF version you can download directly from the product website. Simply create a notebook called "Product Manuals," download a backup file of all your purchases and store them on Evernote.

This is yet another way to move closer to a paperless lifestyle.

Idea #27: Schedule Google Calendar Events

Use IFTTT (*If This, Then That*) to automatically create a new note for each item that goes into Google Calendar: https://ifttt.com/recipes/127362. This is also a great place to add some additional notes about the upcoming event.

The benefit of this hack is you can create an alarm that goes off on your smartphone when an important event is coming up. In my opinion, this is a way better method than an email reminder because you don't have to remember to check your email to get that reminder.

Idea #28: Declutter Your Inbox

Anyone who has an interest in time management understands the danger of an out-of-control email inbox. Fortunately, there's a lot you can do with Evernote to stem the tide.

- Forward your email to Evernote and manage everything in one central location.
- Create a "Delegate" Notebook for identifying recurring requests someone else can handle.

- Create an "Eliminate" Notebook of recurring messages that truly aren't important. Find a way to get rid of them.
- Use free time to write down "template responses" for common requests.

Out-of-control email is the bane of existence for many people. To get better at managing email, you need to practice the daily habit of identifying different areas to streamline.

Idea #29: Write Actionable To-Do Lists

Sometimes a project doesn't require an elaborate list. Instead, you can boil it down into a few simple steps to complete in a short amount of time. With Evernote, you can use the checkbox feature to create a simple list and then use the list to work your way through a project.

It may seem a little silly, but the empty checkbox often becomes a great motivator, prompting you to take action and complete each item quickly.

Idea #30: Share Meeting Notes with Others

You have to be a premium member to edit other people's notes, but anyone can share notes on a "read-only" basis. This is important if you need check out someone else's meeting notes or share yours if a co-worker or boss needs a fast update.

Idea #31: Create Book Notes

Jot down your favorite quotes, comments and any questions you have while reading. Categorize tags according to non-fiction, fiction, classics, business, productivity, etc.

One trick is to add "your highlights" from a Kindle book to a note. The best way to access the "your highlights" section is to log in to see your purchases on kindle.amazon.com. Find the title of the book and pull the highlights directly from this page. From there, it's a simple matter of cutting and pasting the content directly into a note, which will save you the hassle of transcribing.

Idea #32: Create a Networking Database

This is an excellent way to build a database of information on people you've met.

Take pictures of people's business cards and save them to a notebook designed specifically for networking. After you save the cards, insert information about your conversations and why you added each person to the database. You should also set a reminder to follow up with each person at a later date. Enhance your networking efforts by adding personal information such as birthdays, hobbies and spouses' names.

If you follow up with a person six months later, that person will be impressed when you are able to bring up a tiny detail from your first conversation. Evernote makes it easy to keep track of these details and review them before meetings.

Idea #33: Read Articles without Distraction

Use the app Evernote Clearly (http://evernote.com/clearly/) to save all of your Web browsing to a "to-read" list so you don't spend your work time reading articles that aren't relevant to your current projects. The benefit of using Clearly is being able to read each article without the banners and advertisements that often distract us from finishing content in a timely manner.

Idea #34: Archive Whiteboard Notes

Whiteboard sessions are often an essential part of business success because you get to brainstorm a lot of great ideas. You can either whiteboard with a team or do it by yourself, but the problem with this strategy is you'll often need to look at an issue *multiple times* before something clicks.

With Evernote, you can take a quick snapshot of an ongoing whiteboard session and have it accessible at all times. This is perfect if you ever need to remember what was discussed or if you're mapping out a similar idea in the future.

Idea #35: Keep Up with Your Favorite Websites

Sync your favorite RSS reader (like Feedly) to Evernote to have content from your favorite websites sent directly to Evernote. This is yet another way to review content during your downtime.

Idea #36: Keep Copies of Everything You Sign

One of the most important habits to develop is keeping a copy of every document you've ever signed. If there is ever any discrepancy or issue, then you have copies of originals you can pull up within a few minutes. This is an especially important practice if you run a business that requires you to maintain good records.

My advice is to create a Notebook called "Signed Documents" inside a stack called "Personal" and upload every important document you've signed.

Idea #37: Scan Your Receipts

Keeping your receipts is a good financial practice, especially if you run a business and can take business deductions on your tax return. Most of us remember to keep receipts for the big purchases, but the smaller things often slip through the cracks—like the $5 you spent at the post office sending a legal document. If you're doing a good job saving every receipt, you might be drowning in shoeboxes full of paperwork.

Evernote is the perfect tool for scanning and storing receipts. The trick is developing the habit of taking a picture *every time* you get a receipt, no matter how small the expense (or set aside time a few days a week to do this). With a few good tags and the OCR feature of Evernote, you will be able to find any receipt you need within just a few minutes.

In most cases, you need to keep seven years' worth of receipts for tax purposes. That's a lot of paperwork to store in a closet, basement or attic. With Evernote, you can digitize everything and store it all in the cloud.

Idea #38: Collect Tax-Related Documents

In addition to collecting receipts, you can use Evernote to collect paperwork that will be important during tax season. Examples include charitable donation receipts, specific tax forms, proof of business expenses, meeting minutes and contact information for your independent contractors. Ultimately, you need to digitize every piece of paper that deals with the financial aspects of your business.

Many people fear being audited by the IRS. Creating a "Tax Records" notebook and uploading digital copies of your files will help you keep tax information organized. If you're ever audited, it will be easy to defend yourself because you've maintained copies of your paperwork.

Idea #39: Monitor Potential Investments

You might discover a good stock market tip while reading the newspaper, watching a television show on investing or talking with friends. The hard part is remembering to take action on it.

Simply create a notebook called "Potential Investments," then regularly add notes to it. Later on, you can follow up with your financial advisor or check E-Trade or Yahoo! Finance to find out if the potential investment is really worth your money.

Idea #40: Store Photos for Insurance Purposes

If you've ever made an insurance claim for a damaged or stolen item, then you understand the importance of documenting the value of your belongings. My advice? Take photographs of all your valuables to show they're in good working order. Add these photos to Evernote to keep them organized.

Generally speaking, I'd only worry about items worth more than $100. That way, it won't be hard to create a folder full of insurance photos in a single weekend.

Idea #41: Track Spending Throughout the Day

You probably understand the importance of tracking your spending and maintaining a daily budget. Unfortunately, this is often hard to do a day-to-day basis because you're not always in a place where it makes sense to open up a spreadsheet.

Instead, create a notebook called "!DailyExpenses" to use as a temporary stopgap during the day. Then at night, take these notes and insert them into your spending spreadsheet.

Idea #42: Clip Product Reviews and Specs

In my opinion, you should do thorough research before purchasing big-ticket items such as televisions, furniture and fine jewelry. With the Web Clipper add-on, Evernote is the perfect place to put all this research into a comprehensive note.

Include information such as product specs (i.e. size, software compatibility, color), Amazon reviews (what customers did or didn't like about the item), *Consumer Reports* reviews and prices on different websites. Then use this information to make an informed decision about what to buy and how to get the best deal.

Idea #43: Reminders for Bills

Most of your bills have different due dates, so often it's hard to keep track of what needs to be paid. With Evernote, you can use the "alarm" feature to send a notification whenever an important payment is coming up.

You don't necessarily have to do this with every bill. Instead, set reminders for important items such as your rent/mortgage payment, credit cards and utilities.

Idea #44: Collect Automotive Details

Whether you plan on selling your car in the near future or running it into the ground, it's important to maintain repair and service records. Use CamScanner to digitize each bill, write down specific repair/service dates and keep an ongoing list of what you've spent.

Similarly, take pictures of the license plates, the VIN number, car paint colors, tire details, and any specific parts your car needs. This makes it easy to find the answer to any automotive question that might come up.

Idea #45: Collect Home Maintenance Records

Keeping home maintenance records in one place gives you a good history of what has been done and what needs to be fixed in the future. For instance, some roofs need to be replaced about every 20 to 30 years, so you should know the last time your roof was replaced.

Keeping detailed records also helps when it's time to sell your home. You can easily add each note from a "Home Repairs" notebook to a Word document and print them all out. As a result, the new owner will get an accurate record of what's been done with the house.

Idea #46: Create a Vacation Bucket List

Big vacations are often planned well in advance. Sure, you might not be able to book a trip to Japan in 2015, but it might be a place you'd like to visit within the next five years.

In Evernote, you can create a notebook filled with all the travel destinations on your bucket list. Each location should get its own notebook. Here you can add a variety of things: photographs of amazing locations, country-specific travel tips, possible itineraries and once-in-a-lifetime events you should be aware of when you plan your trip.

Idea #47: Create a Travel Itinerary

Using Web Clipper, you can collect important pieces of information for your next trip and put everything in a single notebook. This includes information such as tour details, directions, addresses, hotel reservations, flight information, great restaurants and links to related websites.

As an example, right around the time I'm publishing this book (July 2014), I'm going on a three-week trip to Italy. Naturally, I have a notebook called "Italy 2014," which includes key information on the various places that I'm visiting: Venice, Bolzano, Florence and Cinque Terre. Each is filled with all the information related to that destination. Then when I'm traveling, if I have a question about a place, I can pull up Evernote and immediately find it.

Idea #48: Maintain a Standard Packing List

Is there anything more annoying than forgetting an item during a trip? You can prevent this by creating a standard packing list and storing it in Evernote.

Before leaving, go through this list and pack one thing at a time. Check each item off your list as you add it to your suitcase or duffel bag. This simple system is a great way to ensure you never again leave behind an important item.

Idea #49: Clip Restaurant Ideas

With sites like Yelp (http://yelp.com) and Trip Advisor (http://www.tripadvisor.com/), you can quickly discover great places to eat in *any* part of the world. Once you book a hotel, go to these two sites and use Web Clipper to grab the top-rated restaurants in the area and save them all in a single note. Then when you need a place to eat, you'll instantly have a list of different ideas.

Idea #50: Create a Wiki for Your Travel

This one is for the super-nerdy people (like me). When traveling to a new place, pull basic information from Wikipedia or a travel page and put it into a single note. The benefit to this idea is you develop a better appreciation for a destination when you understand its people, history and culture.

Idea #51: Scan Travel Receipts

Even when traveling, it's important to keep track of your receipts (you never know when these might be important). I'll admit this isn't a fun activity to do on vacation, but you really only need to do this once a week to create digital receipts. Heck, you can even do this poolside while sipping a margarita.

Idea #52: Take Pictures of Important Items

Things often get lost while traveling: luggage, passports, cameras and wallets, to name a few. By storing pictures of your important items in Evernote, you will have a backup just in case anything gets lost, damaged or stolen.

As an example, I once lost my backpack on a trip to Madrid and had a *very* hard time explaining what it looked like in my broken Tarzan-like Spanish. I could have solved this problem very quickly if I had a picture of the backpack stored in Evernote (or if I spoke better Spanish).

Idea #53: Create a Travel Diary

Putting your photos, sketches and thoughts into a note is a great way to create an interactive travel dairy. You could also add short videos and audio recordings to give you a multimedia reminder of your favorite travel memories.

My suggestion is to create a notebook for each major trip and an individual note for each of the individual destinations. That way you won't wonder – years down the road – why you had your head in a tiger's mouth and where this actually happened.

Idea #54: Keep a Reference List

This is great idea for errands and shopping trips. Create a list of favorite brands, clothing sizes and products your family members use. This is useful if you want to surprise someone important with a gift (such as a new shirt) and you can't quite remember their measurements or preferences.

Keep adding notes to this list and you'll quickly build a database of everything that's important.

Idea #55: Create a Gift Idea Database

Sometimes getting a gift requires more knowledge than simply remembering someone's size and personal preferences. If you pay close attention to the people in your life, they probably talk about things they'd like to buy. Inside Evernote, you can start a notebook called "Gift Ideas" where you clip website items and write down random ideas that often pop up during conversations.

Moreover, you can regularly take these ideas and search Amazon for any bargains. This is a great way to get a gift for someone without breaking the bank.

Idea #56: Create a Spiritual Guide

You can use Evernote to collect a variety of inspirational passages, affirmations and quotes. It really doesn't matter *what* you believe in; it's not hard to find something you find uplifting. Put these in a notebook and you'll have content that instantly makes you feel better if you're facing personal challenges.

Idea #57: Build an Evernote Cookbook

Evernote is the perfect tool for building a personal cookbook. Unlike Pinterest and similar sites, you don't have to wade through pages of content to find a specific recipe. Instead, you tag each note with the main ingredients or the meal course (i.e. dinner, desserts and appetizers) to create an easy-to-navigate cookbook.

There are so many ways to create your own cookbook with Evernote.

- Digitize old family recipes.
- Clip an unusual dish you see on Pinterest.
- Snap photos at a fancy restaurant and look for the recipe online.
- Search your favorite cooking site for inspiration.

I'll admit there are a *lot* of recipes out there. The benefit of putting everything into Evernote is you're building a database of what *you* like. Then when you're stuck on what to cook, simply open up your "Recipes" notebook to discover a variety of ideas.

Idea #58: Journal Your Thoughts

Many people use daily journaling as a way to reduce stress and bring order to a hectic lifestyle. You can gain clarity on your day-to-day activities by writing down responses to a few basic questions:

- What are you grateful for?
- What would make today great?
- What interesting things happened to you today?

The questions themselves aren't that important. What's important is creating a simple template you use on a daily basis. This template should act as a prompt for your journaling habit. Do some journaling for a few minutes every day to gain more perspective on what's truly important in your life.

Idea #59: Practice "Extreme Couponing"

I am not an expert couponer by any means. That said, I know there is a specific strategy for leveraging coupons and getting the best possible discount.

While researching this book, I searched Google for "Evernote Couponing" and was surprised at the sheer number of hacks and shortcuts people use in conjunction with Evernote. My suggestion? Spend an afternoon going through these articles to learn how you can save money as well.

Idea #60: Build a "Special Bargains" Notebook

You often hear about special bargains from a variety of sources: friends, neighbors, email, radio and television. For example, a friend might tell you about a one-day sales event at your favorite clothing store. The trick to receiving these discounts is remembering when they happen.

Maximize your savings by creating a note, writing down the date/time and setting a reminder for each event (I recommend setting it for a few days ahead of time). Then you'll be instantly updated when the sale is about to happen.

Idea #61: Become a House Hunter

Searching for a big purchase (such as a home) can be a lengthy process. With Evernote, you can simplify this process in many ways:

- Clip listings and maps of areas you're visiting.

- Create a list of requirements for your ideal home. Use this as a checklist during each open house.

- Put all scheduled appointments, open houses and phone numbers into a single document for easy reference.

- Keep records of the averages for each town: property taxes, median income, prices of homes for your income bracket and any additional costs (e.g. sewage or water).

- Take many photos of the interiors and exteriors of the homes you visit. Attach these photos to a note with the checklists of your likes and dislikes. This makes it easy to keep the facts straight about each house.

Keep these notes for your house-hunting efforts (or any other major purchases) and you'll have enough information to make a well-informed purchasing decision.

Idea #62: Create a Standard Food Shopping List

We're all creatures of habit. There's a good chance you tend to buy the same items over and over when you shop for groceries. The challenge? It's not easy to remember everything you need. A quick solution is to create a standardized food shopping list.

Simply create a checklist of the items you regularly purchase. Then check off what you need before leaving the house and check them off again (in a second box) as buy them. This makes it super simple to remember everything you need.

Remember the Milk is a great app that's very useful for shopping. Visit https://www.rememberthemilk.com/services/evernote/to

learn how to combine this app with Evernote to sync your checklists.

Idea #63: Create a Restaurant "Wish List"

Many people tend to frequent the same few restaurants around their homes. Even if each restaurant is comfortable and serves good food, sometimes it's great to experiment with new places.

Make it easier to experiment by creating a restaurant "wish list" in Evernote. Just like you would do while traveling, use Yelp and Trip Advisor to clip reviews, locations and recommended dishes. Put this information in a single notebook to create a database of ideas for when you want to try something new instead of the same old meal.

Idea #64: Create a Journal of Culinary Experiences

Take pictures of food, leave reviews and share your meal experiences via social media. All of this is possible with the special community that Evernote has created: http://evernote.com/food/

Idea #65: Delay Your Buying Impulses

It's fun to buy new things, but we often can't afford these purchases. One of the psychological reasons we make these impulsive decisions is a fear of loss instead of a desire to gain. For instance, it's easy to feel anxious if you feel like you'll miss out on a "special discount."

You can minimize this problem by taking pictures or making notes on something you want, then storing the information in Evernote. This gives you a "cooling down" period before pulling the trigger. If you really want the item, you can buy it a week later. If the impulse fades, you'll save some cash.

Additionally, you can use this time to do a bit of product research to make sure you're *actually* getting a good deal and purchasing the right thing.

Idea #66: Brainstorm Date Ideas

It's hard to think of creative date ideas. The old "dinner and a movie" date can quickly become repetitive. Evernote is a great tool for keeping track of all the unique or interesting ideas you find.

First, you should regularly read local papers and magazines to find events that are within an hour's drive. Keep track of upcoming concerts, festivals, seasonal events, athletic events and outdoor locations such as state or national parks. Create a note with the particulars of each event (hours, dates, location and type of event) within a "Date Ideas" notebook.

Next, create a timeline of these events. Set a reminder if the idea can only be done on a certain day.

Finally, review the Date Ideas notebook on a regular basis—at least every other week. If you can plan these activities in advance, never again will you be forced to sit through a boring "dinner and movie" date.

Idea #67: Remember Every Song

Have you ever heard a song you like but can't figure out the title or how to find it? What you can do is make an audio recording of the song and save it to Evernote. Then when you have spare time, use an app such as ***Shazam*** (http://www.shazam.com/music/web/getshazam.html) to discover the specifics of the song and find out where to buy it.

Idea #68: Clip Song Lyrics.

Words can be inspirational—even the lyrics from your favorite songs. You can clip and collect certain verses and put them into a single note. Then whenever you feel down, open this note to remember what lifts your spirits.

Each note can also act as a reminder for songs that make you happy. Add each to a Spotify (http://www.spotify.com) playlist to improve your mood.

Idea #69: Be Social

Twitter and Facebook are integrated with Evernote. Not only can you import a Twitter feed directly into the app, you can also easily share a note with your friends, family members and followers. This strategy is great if you want to build buzz for a current project you're putting together.

Idea #70: Build a Medical History

If you've ever been a new patient at a doctor's office (or have to go to the hospital), then you know they ask *a lot* of questions about your medical history. You can simplify things by creating a note for each of the following:

- Data from previous checkups (i.e. weight, blood pressure, blood sugar levels)
- Medical histories of your family members with important milestone dates
- Dates and descriptions of previous visits
- Journal of any illness-related symptoms

You need to fill out a lot of paperwork during a medical visit, so keeping all these notes will help minimize the stress of remembering dozens of dates and numbers.

Idea #71: Archive Your Prescriptions

Another medical note to add is a list of your past and current prescriptions. Include pharmacy receipts, prescription slips, doctor contact information, exact dosages and instructions for how to take each medication. You should also schedule reminders for when a prescription needs to be refilled.

Idea #72: Write in a Food Journal

The benefit of a food journal is the ability to track what you eat on a daily basis. This helps you stick with a specific diet and gain insight about what you're *actually* eating. Yes, there are lots of "food journal apps" that do the same thing. However, some people like to keep everything in Evernote and avoid having to update multiple apps.

Idea #73: Build a Genealogy Database

Genealogy requires a painstaking amount of research into birth certificates, death records, immigration documents, family trees, census records, old family photos, interviews with relatives and other supporting paperwork. While you should always keep physical copies of these items, you should also keep backups within Evernote.

Idea #74: Track Quarterly (or Yearly) Goals

Goal setting has been proven to be a critical part of personal success. When you write down actionable goals and review them daily, you increase your chances of actually achieving them. A great way to use Evernote is to create a list of five to seven goals you'd like to accomplish in the near future.

My advice is to create a notebook called !Goals, which will put the notebook near the top of your dashboard.

Inside this notebook, create an individual note filled with your goals for the next three months. (I prefer quarterly goals over yearly goals because they feel more immediate and important.) Then open up this note on a daily basis and review each goal.

Idea #75: De-Clutter Your Life

By now, you probably see how Evernote can help de-clutter your life. It does the following:

- Organizes your digital life by creating central location for all your important paperwork, files and documents.
- Replaces bulky filing cabinets.
- Acts as a substitute for bulky items such as cookbooks and travel guides.
- Eliminates the need to print out reference materials.
- Creates a backup for all product warranties and documentation.
- Creates checklist processes for regular cleaning activities.

While Evernote doesn't magically clean your home for you, it can be used as a tool to better organize your home. You'll find that once you've developed the habit of digitizing certain items, you'll start to eliminate a lot of clutter you really don't need.

Picking YOUR Ideas

These are just 75 ideas for getting started with Evernote. Should you try all of them at once? Definitely not. This app is like any other tool—the more it's used, the more you'll need it on a daily basis. Don't worry if this previous list seems like a lot to do. My recommendation is to think of your biggest "problem" areas and use Evernote to solve them.

For instance, consider the challenges you face on a daily basis. Do you struggle to get things done? Are you buried under an avalanche of paperwork? Do you often forget certain items at the grocery store? Having trouble going from an idea to a completed project?

Evernote can help you fix all of these problems. To a certain degree, each one requires you to store notes, record ideas, flesh out projects and create simple checklists. If you commit to using this app on a daily basis, you'll quickly find a number of unique ways to use it.

Our time together is almost at an end. In the last section, we'll talk about 15 apps and add-ons that work perfectly with Evernote.

15 "Must-Have" Add-Ons for Evernote

Throughout this book, we've talked about different add-ons that bring an extra level of functionality to Evernote. In this section, I'll cover 15 of my favorites. What's important here is most of the following apps are owned by Evernote instead of a third party, so you know they'll work seamlessly within the app. Third-party companies work closely with the Evernote team to ensure their apps give the end user a positive experience.

I know we've already talked about a few of these add-ons, but I think it's important to include them all in one section so you know which apps you should download right away.

First, let's start with the three apps that are almost a "core" part of the Evernote experience:

#1. Evernote Web Clipper (http://evernote.com/webclipper/)(clip Web articles)

#2. Evernote Clearly (http://evernote.com/clearly/) (read content later without advertisements or distractions)

#3. Skitch (http://evernote.com/skitch/) (clip and mark up images)

You already know about these three tools, so let's move on to the others we haven't talked about at length:

#4. Evernote Hello: http://evernote.com/hello/

Your brain doesn't file information about the people you meet in a tidy, alphabetical order. It categorizes each person by face and by where, when and *how* you met someone. With Evernote Hello, you create and search for people based on the circumstances of where you established the relationship (e.g. "husband's high school reunion"). This is a great tool if you do a lot of networking and meet many different people on a regular basis.

#5. Evernote Food: http://evernote.com/food/

With Evernote Food, you can review food choices, share recipes, find culinary ideas, read restaurant reviews and document your favorite dishes. Everything you could possibly need to improve your "foodie lifestyle" can be found and saved with this Evernote add-on.

#6 Penultimate: http://evernote.com/penultimate/

I was tempted to put this in the "must-have" section because it's something most people will use from time to time. Penultimate helps you enter information into Evernote using good old-fashioned handwriting. This is a perfect way to add drawings, idea sketches or school notes to your Evernote account.

#7. Shoeboxed:
https://www.shoeboxed.com/partner/evernote/

This app will help you digitize and keep track of mounds of paperwork, receipts and business cards. In other words, using it is the first step to eliminating all the clutter you normally keep in a shoebox. If you want to go paperless, then this app can help you get started.

#8. News 360: http://blog.news360.com/2012/06/news360-connected-evernote/

Our lives are busy, and searching the Web for headlines often takes up too much time. With News 360, you get a service that delivers specific news items to match your personal interests.

#9. Evernote Peek: http://evernote.com/peek/

This app can immediately replace flash cards as your preferred study tool. The answers are covered by a virtual or real cover that shows *only* the question, then reveals the answer to show you if you're correct. This add-on provides yet another "hack" for using Evernote in all aspects of your life.

#10. DocuSign: https://appcenter.evernote.com/app/docusign/iphone

Save important files, get signatures right on your mobile device and then send the information right back to Evernote. This add-on gives you a simple way to keep track of all your important legal documents.

#11 FileThis: https://filethis.com/

The "FileThis" software grabs your online statements, bills and other financial documents from companies such as Amazon, MasterCard and Chase so you don't have to log in to these accounts whenever you want to check something. When used with Evernote, you'll have a single place to store all of your billing information.

When I reviewed this app, I was concerned about the level of security with this tool, so I'd definitely look into purchasing the encryption option to make sure your financial information is fully protected.

#12. Azendoo:
http://appcenter.evernote.com/app/azendoo/web-apps

Azendoo is a task management app that can be used for collaborative team projects and managing specific tasks.

#13. I Health – My Vitals:
http://appcenter.evernote.com/app/ihealth-myvitals/iphone

Use this app for iPhone to help you track blood pressure, body fat percentages, calories consumed and food intake. All of this can be stored in one central location within Evernote.

#14. CamScanner: https://www.CamScanner.net/

This is yet another add-on that I considered adding to the "must-have" group. The ability to take pictures and scan them into a PDF file gives you a simple solution for creating a paperless lifestyle. Even if you have a quality scanner at home, this app offers the same solution if you're constantly on the go.

#15. Pocket Informant:
http://appcenter.evernote.com/app/pocket-informant/iphone

This app acts as an all-in-one calendar, task manager and organizational tool. It is set up to fully sync with Evernote as its primary database. If you're into the *Getting Things Done* approach for productivity, then this is a great tool to use in conjunction with Evernote.

Conclusion

I'll admit it...I didn't really "get" Evernote at first. On the surface, it seemed like a glorified to-do list manager and idea capture device. However, it wasn't until I put the app through its paces that I discovered its power and the many ways it can be used to improve my life. Now? I don't know what I'd do without the Evernote app.

You might feel a bit overwhelmed after reading this book. Because there's a lot you can do with Evernote, you might be unsure of how to get started. Don't worry if this sounds like you. A great thing about this tool is it's easy to use right out of the box. You can do the basic things without getting sidetracked by the advanced features. Then if you want to "do more," you can add a multitude of apps and incorporate the higher-level stuff.

As we close things out, I suggest doing a few things to get started.

First, download the Evernote app on all the devices you use—if you haven't done so already. I encourage you to play around with the core functions.

Create stacks for the major areas of your life: work, health, family, travel, finances and future projects. Inside each stack, add notebooks that break down content into specific categories. For instance, inside the finance stack you could create notebooks such as *Tax Records, Receipts* and *Investments*. Finally, add notes within each specific notebook to keep track of important information.

Next, spend a few hours building a collection of tags. These will become your shortcut for locating any piece of content, so it makes sense to create 100 to 200 tags that represent the different areas of your life.

Third, download the three apps that work seamlessly with Evernote. They are Evernote Web Clipper (http://evernote.com/webclipper/), Evernote Clearly (http://evernote.com/clearly/) and Skitch (http://evernote.com/skitch/). If you're feeling adventurous, add the other apps included on my list of 15 suggestions.

After that, think of the different types of notes you can add to Evernote. You don't have to use all 75 of the ideas in this book, nor do you need to stick to just this list. Just think of the areas of your life that need the most help and start using Evernote to minimize problem areas.

Finally, when you get comfortable with the app, try using some of the advanced strategies in this book. Go to IFTTT.com to set up Evernote-specific recipes. Use Skitch to mark up images on the fly. Create a *Getting Things Done* system for your personal productivity. Save important emails as notes.

As you've learned, Evernote is a simple app that's capable of doing so much more than advertised. I encourage you to test out the many strategies discussed throughout this book. Don't be afraid to make mistakes— that's the best way to learn something. The more time you invest in this tool, the more you will benefit from using it on a daily basis.

The great thing about Evernote is it's a useful tool whether you use it to organize your personal life or to create a successful business. It's also easy to blend your personal and professional lives by using Evernote to store recipes, networking details, shopping lists, to-do lists, professional goals and other important information. Download Evernote now to see how well it can work for you.

S.J. Scott
Author: http://www.HabitBooks.com
Blog: http://www.DevelopGoodHabits.com

Would You Like to Know More?

You can learn a lot more about habit development in my other Kindle books. The best part? I frequently run special promotions where I offer free or discounted books (usually $0.99) on Amazon.

One way to get <u>instant notifications</u> for these deals is to subscribe to my email list. By joining not only will you receive updates on the latest offer, you'll also get a free copy of my book "77 Good Habits to Live a Better Life." Check out the below link to learn more.

<u>http://www.developgoodhabits.com/free-updates</u>

Thank You

Before you go, I'd like to say "thank you" for purchasing my guide.

I know you could have picked from dozens of books on habit development, but you took a chance with my system.

So a big thanks for ordering this book and reading all the way to the end.

Now I'd like ask for a *small* favor. **Could you please take a minute or two and leave a review for this book on Amazon?**

This feedback will help me continue to write the kind of books that help you get results. And if you loved it, then please let me know :-)

More Books by S.J. Scott

- *Habit Stacking: 97 Small Life Changes That Take Five Minutes Or Less*

- *To-Do List Makeover: A Simple Guide to Getting the Important Things Done*

- *23 Anti-Procrastination Habits: How to Stop Being Lazy and Get Results In Your Life*

- *S.M.A.R.T. Goals Made Simple: 10 Steps to Master Your Personal and Career Goals*

- *Writing Habit Mastery: How to Write 2,000 Words a Day and Forever Cure Writer's Block*

- *Declutter Your Inbox: 9 Proven Steps to Eliminate Email Overload*

- *Wake Up Successful: How to Increase Your Energy and Achieve Any Goal with a Morning Routine*

- *10,000 Steps Blueprint: The Daily Walking Habit for Healthy Weight Loss and Lifelong Fitness*

- *70 Healthy Habits: How to Eat Better, Feel Great, Get More Energy and Live a Healthy Lifestyle*

- *Resolutions That Stick! How 12 Habits Can Transform Your New Year*

About the Author

"Build a Better Life - One Habit at a Time"

Getting more from life doesn't mean following the latest diet craze or motivation program. True success happens when you take action on a daily basis. In other words, it's your habits that help you achieve goals and live the life you've always wanted.

In his books, S.J. provides daily action plans for every area of your life: health, fitness, work and personal relationships. Unlike other personal development guides, his content focuses on taking action. So instead of reading over-hyped strategies that rarely work in the real-world, you'll get information that can be immediately implemented

When not writing, S.J. likes to read, exercise and explore the different parts of the world.